T0332310

Self-Portrait in the Studio

THE ITALIAN LIST

Giorgio Agamben
Self-Portrait in the Studio

TRANSLATED BY KEVIN ATTELL

LONDON NEW YORK CALCUTTA

THE ITALIAN LIST
Series Editor: Alberto Toscano

This book has been translated thanks to a translation grant awarded by the Italian Ministry of Foreign Affairs and International Cooperation.

Questo libro è stato tradotto grazie a un contributo alla traduzione assegnato dal Ministero degli Affari Esteri e della Cooperazione Internazionale italiano.

Seagull Books, 2024

First published in Italian as *Autoritratto nello studio*
© nottetempo srl, Milan, 2017

First published in English translation by Seagull Books, 2024
English translation © Kevin Attell, 2024

ISBN 978 1 80309 465 6

British Library Cataloguing-in-Publication Data
A catalogue record for this book is available from the British Library

Typeset by Seagull Books, Calcutta, India
Printed and bound in the USA by Integrated Books International

CONTENTS

1

Self-Portrait in the Studio

173

Translator's Notes

177

List of Illustrations

Threshold

The self-portraits of painters—Bonnard's and Arikha's, as they are painting in the studio, so ardent and unforgiving; Tintoretto's and Titian's, painted with their own ashes—Gaugin's self-portrait près du Golgotha *in the Marquesas—he is not exactly old, but it is clear that he has seen too much—horror as well—and wants to see no more—now, you can say what your eyes have seen only by depicting your gaze, unyieldingly, in a sort of stupor—completely disillusioned, disenchanted.*

It is not possible to reach anything like this in writing, such an extreme and lucid fog, such a steadfast feeling about oneself.

The doors of the mystery allow one to enter, but they do not allow one to leave. The moment comes when we know we have crossed that threshold, and little by little we realize that we will never be able to go back out. Not that the mystery deepens, on the contrary—we simply know that we will never come out of it again.

When a door is no longer a door.

Like perfection; without lament.
One becomes so lucid that one goes mad.
Transforming one's own idiotisms into prayers and praying continuously.

It is said that the old have only one string left to play. And it is perhaps an untuned string that produces what Stefano used to call the 'wolf's note'. But that single untuned string sounds more fully and deeply than the whole instrument of youth.

Being at home in being lost. The only sure thing is that we no longer know where we truly are. Or better: we feel that we are at a point, that we are this point, this 'where'—but we no longer know how to locate it in space and time. All the places where we have lived, all the moments we have lived through besiege us and ask to come in—we watch them, we recall them one by one—from where? Where *is everywhere and nowhere. Becoming* intimately *foreign to ourselves—with neither fatherland nor motherland. All that we have—habits, clothes, memories—there are too many of them; we cannot have them any more.*

How near it is now, the unreachable!

A crab holding a butterfly aloft in its claws.

'*The heaven is creaking and it should creak, for there is no space in it the width of four fingers but there is an angel there.*'[1] *While all of our faculties seem to diminish and fail us, the imagination grows to excess and takes up all possible space. And no longer is it something distinct from reality; rather, reality shatters into images that the imagination ceaselessly gathers. Desires so fully imagined that they can no longer be satisfied.*

Astonishment that hope may remain intact, even in the certain knowledge that it will not be fulfilled, that only the unfulfillable is real.

The themes of life—it now seems that you can nearly hear them, as in a musical score. Decisive meetings, friendships, loves are the phrases and motifs that call and respond in the secret counterpoint of existence, which has no staff on which to write them down. And even when they seem to lie in a remote past, the themes of life are necessarily unfinished, like an interrupted melody or fugue that waits to be finished and taken up again. Try to listen to them—in the dark. Nothing else.

It is like watching something at dusk. It is not so much that the light is uncertain but that you know you will not be able to finish seeing because the light will fade. This is how things and people now appear: fixed forever in the impossibility of seeing them to the end.

Sub quondam caducitatis specie. *And this alone is eternal.*

It is the moment when we feel we no longer can nor want to have anything. Want only to clear away, make space—but it is already too late even for this.

Tardus *means slow. But there is a special quickness of those who know it is nevertheless too late* [tardi].

Praesto *means 'near, within reach'. Is 'late', then, what our hands will never be able to reach?*

A form of life that keeps itself in relation to a poetic practice, however that might be, is always in the studio, always in its studio.

(*Its*—but in what way do that place and practice belong to it? Isn't the opposite true—that this form of life is at the mercy of its studio?)

In the mess of papers and books, open or piled upon one another, in the disordered scene of brushes and paints, canvases leaning against the wall, the studio preserves the rough drafts of creation; it records the traces of the arduous process leading from potentiality to act, from the hand that writes to the written page, from the palette to the painting. The studio is the image of potentiality—of the writer's potentiality to write, of the painter's or sculptor's potentiality to paint or sculpt. Attempting to describe one's own studio thus means attempting to describe the modes and forms of one's own potentiality—a task that is, at least on first glance, impossible.

How does one have a potentiality? One cannot have a potentiality; one can only inhabit it.

Habito is a frequentative of *habeo*: to inhabit is a special mode of having, a having so intense that it is no longer possession at all. By dint of having something, we inhabit it, we belong to it.

The objects of my studio have remained the same, and years later in the photographs of them in different places and cities, they seem unchanged. The studio is the form of its inhabiting—how could it change?

In the wicker letter tray against the wall at the centre of the desk in both my studio in Rome and the one in Venice, on the left there is an invitation to the dinner celebrating Jean Beaufret's seventieth birthday, on the front of which is written this line from Simone Weil: 'Un homme qui a quelque chose de nouveau à dire ne peut être d'abord écouté que de ceux qui l'aiment.'[2] The invitation carries the date 22 May 1977. Since then, it has always remained on my desk.

One knows something only if one loves it—or, as Elsa would say, 'only one who loves knows'. The Indo-European root that means

'to know' is a homonym for the one that means 'to be born'. To know [*conoscere*] means to be born [*nascere*] together, to be generated or regenerated by the thing known. This, and nothing but this, is the meaning of loving. And yet, it is precisely this type of love that is so difficult to find among those who believe they know. In fact, the opposite often occurs—that those who dedicate themselves to the study of a writer or an object end up developing a feeling of superiority towards them, even a sort of contempt. This is why it is best to expunge from the verb 'to know' all merely cognitive claims (*cognitio* in Latin is originally a legal term meaning the procedures for a judge's inquiry). For my own part, I do not think we can pick up a book we love without feeling our heart racing, or truly know a creature or thing without being reborn in them and with them.

The photograph with Heidegger to my left, in my studio on Vicolo del Giglio in Rome, was taken in the countryside of Vaucluse during one of the walks that punctuated the first seminar at Le Thor in 1966. At a distance of half a century, I cannot forget the landscape of Provence immersed in the September light, the white rocks of the bories, the great, steep hump of Mont Ventoux, the ruins of Sade's Château de Lacoste perched on the rocks. And the feverish, star-pierced night sky, which the moist gauze of the Milky Way seemed to want to soothe. It is perhaps the first place I wanted to hide my heart—and there, untouched and unripe as it was, my heart must have remained, even if I could no longer say where—perhaps under a boulder in Saumane, in a hut of Le Rebanqué, or in the garden of the little hotel where Heidegger held his seminar every morning.

What did the meeting with Heidegger in Provence mean to me? I certainly cannot separate it from the place where it happened—his face at once gentle and stern, intense and uncompromising eyes that I have never seen elsewhere save in a dream. In life there are events and meetings that are so decisive that it is impossible for them to enter into reality completely. They happen, to be sure, and they mark out the path—but they never cease to happen, so to speak. Meetings that are, in this sense, *continuous*, as theologians say that God never ceases to create the world, that there is a continuous creation of the world. These meetings never cease to accompany us until the end.

They are part of what remains unfinished in a life, what goes beyond it. And what goes beyond life is what remains of it.

I remember, in the dilapidated church of Thouzon, which we visited on one of our excursions in Vaucluse, the Cathar dove carved inside the architrave of a window in such a way that no one could see it without looking at it from behind.

That small group of people walking together towards Thouzon in the photograph from September 1966—what became of it? Each in his own way had more or less consciously meant to make something of his life—the two seen from the back on the right are René Char and Heidegger, behind them myself and Dominique—what became

of them, what became of us? Two have been dead a long time; the other two are, as they say, getting on in years (getting on towards what?). What matters here is not work, but life. Because on that late sunny afternoon (the shadows are long) they were alive and felt it, each intent in his thoughts, that is, in the bit of good that he had glimpsed. What has become of that good, wherein thought and life were not yet divided, wherein the feeling of the sun on the skin and the shadow of words in the mind so happily merged?

Smara in Sanskrit means both love and memory. We love someone because we remember them and, vice versa, we remember because we love. In loving we remember and in remembering we love, and in the end we love the memory—that is, love itself—and we remember love—that is, memory itself. This is why loving means being unable to forget, being unable to get a face, a gesture, a light out of your mind. But in truth it also means that we can no longer have a memory of it, that love is beyond memory, immemorably, ceaselessly present.

It was José Bergamín who during one of our meetings in Madrid introduced me to Ramón Gaya, who generously lent me the studio on Vicolo del Giglio, where I wrote and lived for about ten years starting in 1978. That my studio had been a painter's studio—as my first studio on Piazza delle Coppelle had been a writer's—and that I always left the easel just as I had found it there, with a newly started painting on it, certainly has something to do with my love for

painting, as if it were being tacitly handed over. I still remember the
ease with which Ramón, who had left the studio two years earlier
for what he thought would be a short trip to Spain, told me I could
use it as I liked. I learned later that he had lost everything during the
Civil War, his house, his paintings, his wife, killed in a fascist bombing
at the station in Barcelona where Ramón was hoping to reach her,
his daughter—miraculously pulled from her mother's arms by two
Englishmen—whom he was able to see again only 15 years later.

Meßkirch, 28. Oktober 1967.

Lieber Herr Agamben,

ich danke Ihnen herzlich für das grossartige Geschenk der van Gogh-Briefe zu meinem Geburtstag. Ich weiß dieses Geschenk der jungen Freunde aus dem Heraklit-Seminar in der Provence sehr wohl zu schätzen. Ich hoffe, dass es uns allen vergönnt sein wird, im kommenden Jahr das Begonnene auf eine fruchtbare Weise fortzusetzen.

Mit herzlichen Grüßen für Sie u. die Freundin

Ihr

Martin Heidegger

Echte Foto, Verlag Karl Göckel, Messkirch

Das Bild zeigt das Tal der oberen Donau, in der Nähe meiner Heimat. Hölderlin hat es dort wandelnd auf seinem Weg nach der Schweiz.

On the wall of Vicolo del Giglio, on the right hang two postcards sent to me by Heidegger, one with a photograph of the Hütte in Todtnauberg, the other with a landscape of the upper Danube. 'The image,' he writes, in his clear hand, the hand of the philosopher, 'shows the valley of the upper Danube in the area near my homeland. Hölderlin crossed it on his trip towards Switzerland.' On the envelope I am almost surprised to read the address of my first studio, Piazza delle Coppelle 48. The two postcards are also in my studio in Venice,

but on another wall. In their place above the desk hang two photographs taken by François Fédier during the seminar of 1968; in one
of them Heidegger appears to be animatedly discussing something
with me and Jean Beaufret, I can't remember what.

In another image published in a French magazine, the caption
reads 'Heidegger and René Char among bocce players.' In that little
square in Le Thor, Heidegger enjoyed watching the locals throwing
their pétanques, but among the people in the photo there are only
two players; the others are members of the 1966 seminar: in addition
to me, there are Beaufret, Vézin and, just barely visible, the young
poet and student of Char, Dominique Fourcade, from whom I first

learned of the seminar. (In another photo that I have, however, the players are quite visible).

At that time, I stood, as another poet wrote, on one foot, enclosed within a chalk circle, longing only to leap out of it and escape. In memory, it is as if I returned to that circle, which instead now seems incredibly happy to me.

(When we are young, our hands do not know what they seek—they perhaps know what they reject, but what they reject forms the negative image of what they seek; in some way it guides them towards the unseen good).

Beyond the one of Thouzon, I do not have any photographs of the Provençal countryside, then still untouched by the ravages of tourism. One image is on a postcard I sent to Giovanni Urbani, which, knowing it would be a pleasant surprise for him, I asked Heidegger to sign. The postcard shows the bories as they then appeared, scattered across the countryside and still sometimes used by the farmers.

So Giovanni was already present in my life. I was 22 years old when I met him, and he, if I remember correctly, was about to turn 40. The Rome of those days, so sweet, reticent and poor, is so far away, almost prehistoric; as I now remember it, it seems divided into two worlds, each built on an unyielding snobbery. The first of these worlds, to which I was introduced by Juan Rodolfo Wilcock, centred around Elsa Morante. In addition to some people my age, it included Pasolini, Sandro Penna, Cesare Garboli and Natalia Ginzburg to varying degrees and in various ways. In the second world, which was more *monde* in the social sense of the term, there were Alberto Arbasino, Ennio Flaiano, Giorgio Bassani, Francesco Rosi and an indeterminate number of creatures, as improbable as they were inaccessible, who belonged to the Roman nobility and 'high society'. The two circles did not mix; in fact, they avoided each other. But there was a third group that gathered around Alberto Moravia whose members were occasionally admitted to both. It was with the second circle, which was much less familiar to me, that one evening I happened to meet Giovanni. His ascetic, legendary elegance, his *sprezzatura*, which was oddly marked by a note of irreducible strangeness, won me over easily. His exacting worldliness notwithstanding, I understood right away that his *daimon* was not Swann, but (as I also later learned from him directly) Lord Jim, that is, a man whose life has a shadow forever cast over it by a wrong he did not truly commit.

In any case, Heidegger, whom I had been reading for a few years and who for Giovanni was the vanishing point on which his reflections on art converged, became 'our' author, a sort of esoteric talisman that no one in Roman culture at the time was able to share.

If I think now of Giovanni in the last years of his life, I once again see the veil of sadness that seemed to cloud his face after he had resigned from the Istituto Centrale di Restauro and, by then separated from Kiki, lived as we dream, alone. Of course, I did not know how to do anything for him; I did not try to question the figure hidden behind that veil, nor do I believe he could have accepted it if I had. The very person who had introduced me to the absence of mystery in life now seemed to wrap himself up in an unconfessable secret. And yet, while he drew further and further away, closed up in his immaculate double-breasted suit and his inscrutable heart, I believe— no, part of me knows with certainty that he remained until the end, like his Conradian alter ego, 'one of us', perhaps unforgivable in his own eyes but to me faithful like no one else to his every gesture and his every word.

Many years later, in 1985, I returned to Le Thor and looked for the hotel where we stayed during the seminar (it was called Le chasselas, named after a local grape variety that makes a very fragrant moscato). When I found myself in front of it, for a moment I did not believe my eyes: it had not changed at all; it was as if I had just left it—as if time in that spot had stopped while everything around it had kept up to date and kept pace with the new necessities and fashions. One minute later I understood why: the hotel had been completely abandoned, the front door hanging off its hinges, the double stairs leading up to it crumbling, the garden where we held the seminar covered with weeds.

So strong was the impression of anachronism that it seemed to me that the abandonment was not a matter of mere chance, as if Le chasselas had been waiting for me all those years, as if that incompleteness and that abandonment were a reflection of my immaturity at that time and my inability to remain faithful to the encounter that had taken place. For if it had been exceedingly happy as far as the senses and that landscape were concerned, with regard to the seminar something had remained unfulfilled or in suspense. To be sure, I read Heidegger intensely and his thought was at the centre of my conversations with Giovanni. And yet, the mind alone is not enough to make an encounter; it requires the heart as well. And my heart in those years was elsewhere, irresolute and uncertain. The union of heart and mind happened to me suddenly—I remember it clearly— in May of 1976, at the precise moment when I heard the news of

Heidegger's death. I felt that I had definitively left perplexity and indecision behind me and my new certainty expressed itself in two gestures: the dedication 'in memoriam Martin Heidegger' of the book I had just finished (*Stanzas*) and the printing of *Prose* in an edition of 50 copies for friends—a sort of farewell to poetry in name of a poetic practice that I would never abandon: philosophy, the 'supreme music'.

During the second seminar at Le Thor, I spoke with Heidegger of Hannah Arendt, whom I had begun to read enthusiastically, and, along with Dominique Fourcade, asked him for her address in New York. But it was only two years later that I found the courage to write to her, including with the letter the essay 'On the Limits of Violence', which I had recently published in *Nuovi Argomenti*. At that moment the question of the legitimacy of violence was especially current in Italy as well, but among the leaders of the movements with whom I would sometimes discuss things, Arendt was considered a reactionary writer because in her book *The Origins of Totalitarianism* she had put soviet totalitarianism and fascism on the same level. Thus, a conception of politics that could have oriented the movements more successfully was shut out of them. If it is true, as Benjamin writes, that every book carries with it a historical index that marks the moment when it should be read, then when those same leaders decided to read her many years later, it was too late: the hour of her legibility had long since passed.

My short essay seems to me now—and maybe already seemed to me then—inadequate, and yet, Hannah Arendt had the generosity to cite it in a note included in the German edition of her book *On Violence*. And I recently learned from the editor of the volume of letters between Mary McCarthy and Nicola Chiaromonte that she had given it to her friend Mary, who, in a letter to Chiaromonte, speaks of it and asks information about its author ('When I went to visit Hannah recently in the Ticino, she gave me something to read for her by a Giorgio Agamben. Who is he?'). Once again, it appears to me that a mysterious connection binds the people who were dear

to me in various ways. Indeed, it had been Giovanni Urbani who had introduced me to Chiaromonte, who edited the journal *Tempo presente*, where my first essays appeared between 1966 and 1967. Chiaromonte, who had fought against the fascists in Spain, was one of the few Italian intellectuals who thought seriously about the relation between man and historical event, between what he believes and what happens to him. 1971 saw the publication of his book *Credere e non credere* (Belief and nonbelief), which raised the question of the problem of faith in our age in history. The sentence that opens the essay 'An Age of Bad Faith' particularly struck me and I believe it has lost none of its truth: 'Ours is not an age of faith, nor is it an age of disbelief. It is an age of bad faith, of beliefs which are clung to in order to oppose other beliefs or which are maintained in the absence of genuine convictions.'[3]

A page from Chiaromonte's notebooks contains an extraordinary meditation on what remains of a life. For him the essential issue is not what we have or have not had—the true question is, rather, 'what remains? . . . what remains of all the days and years that we lived as we could, that is, lived according to a necessity whose law we cannot even now decipher, but *at the same time* lived as it happened, which is to say, by chance?' The answer is that what remains, if it remains, is 'that which one is, that which one was: the memory of having been "beautiful", as Plotinus would say, and the ability to keep it alive even now. Love remains, if one felt it, the enthusiasm for noble actions, for the traces of nobility and valour found in the dross of life. What remains, if it remains, is the ability to hold that what was good was good, what was bad was bad, and that nothing one might do can change that. What remains is what was, what deserves to continue and last, what *stays*.'[4]

The answer seems so clear and forthright that the words that conclude the brief meditation pass unobserved: 'And of us, of that Ego from which we can never detach ourselves and which we can never abjure, nothing remains.' And yet, I believe that these final, quiet words lend sense to the answer that precedes them. The good— even if Chiaromonte insists on its 'staying' and 'lasting'—is not a substance that has no relation to our witnessing of it; rather, only this 'of us nothing remains' guarantees that something good remains. The good is somehow indiscernible from our cancelling ourselves in it; it lives only by the seal and arabesque that our disappearance marks upon it. This is why we cannot detach ourselves from ourselves or abjure ourselves. Who is 'I'? Who are 'we'? Only this vanishing, this holding our breath for something higher that, nevertheless, draws life and inspiration from our bated breath. And nothing says more, nothing is more unmistakably unique than that tacit vanishing, nothing more moving than that adventurous disappearance.

Every life always runs along two levels: one seemingly governed by necessity, even if, as Chiaromonte writes, we cannot decipher its law, and another that is abandoned to chance and contingency. There is no point in pretending there is some arcane, demonic harmony between these two (this is the hypocritical claim that I was never able to accept in Goethe), and yet, once we manage to look at ourselves without disgust, the two levels, though uncommunicating, do not exclude or contrast with each other; rather, they offer each other a sort of serene, reciprocal hospitality. This is the only reason why the thin fabric of our life can slip out of our hands almost imperceptibly, while the facts and events—that is, the errors—that lay its warp attract all our attention and all our useless care.

What accompanies us through life is also what nourishes us. To nourish does not simply mean to make something grow; above all, it means to let something reach the state to which it naturally tends. The meetings, the readings and the places that nourish us help us to reach this state. And yet, something in us resists this maturation and, just when it seems close, stubbornly stops and turns back towards the unripe.

A medieval legend about Virgil, whom popular tradition had turned into a magician, relates that upon realizing he was old he employed his arts to regain his youth. After having given the necessary instructions to a faithful servant, he had himself cut up into pieces, salted and cooked in a cauldron, warning that no one should look inside the pot before it was time. But the servant—or, according to another version, the emperor—opened the pot too soon. 'At that point,' the legend recounts, 'there was seen an entirely naked child who circled three times around the tub containing the meat of Virgil and then vanished and of the poet nothing remained.' Recalling this legend in the *Diapsalmata*, Kierkegaard bitterly comments, 'I dare say that I also peered too soon into the cauldron, into the cauldron of life and the historical process, and most likely will never manage to become more than a child.'[5]

Maturing is letting oneself be cooked by life, letting oneself blindly fall—like a fruit—wherever. Remaining an infant is wanting to open the pot, wanting to see immediately even what you are not supposed to look at. But how can one not feel sympathy for those people in the fables who recklessly open the forbidden door.

In her diaries, Etty Hillesum writes that a soul can be 12 years old forever. This means that our recorded age changes with time but the soul has an age of its own that remains unchanged from birth to death. I don't know the exact age of my soul, but it surely cannot be very old, in any case not more than nine, judging from the way I seem to recognize it in my memories from that age, which have thus remained so vivid and sharp. Every year that passes, the gap between my recorded age and the age of my soul widens, and the feeling of this difference is an ineliminable part of the way I life my life, of both its great imbalances and its precarious equilibriums.

On the middle shelf of the bookcase to the left in the studio on Vicolo del Giglio, you can see a photograph of Herman Melville, who was therefore already particularly important to me by that time.

I have often thought how inadequate it is for him to be categorized exclusively among novelists. It is clear that as a novel *Moby-Dick* is a failure and only the inertia of critics can explain this persistence in

placing it within a literary genre. In truth, it is a *Summa theologica*, the most extraordinary reflection on God that the nineteenth century was capable of, comparable to the 'Grand Inquisitor' and to Ivan Karamazov's description of the devil (it is clear, in any case, that Melville and Dostoyevsky are the greatest theologians of that century so poor in theology).

Only someone familiar with the Kabbalistic *Shi'ur Qomah*, with its description and meticulous measurement of the face of God ('The height of the Creator is 236,000 parasangs and the length of a parasang is 3 miles and a mile is 10,000 armlengths [. . .] The appearance of the face is like the appearance of the cheeks')[6] can understand the minute, mad descriptions of the head and face of the whale in chapters 74–77 and the equally insistent measurements of the length of the cetacean and of every member of its divine body. According to Scholem, the *Shi'ur Qomah* (literally, the 'measure of the body') must have originated with groups of heretical mystics who gathered around the fringes of Rabbinic Judaism and had contacts with gnostic traditions. In any case, these mystics—if such they were—give themselves the impossible task of measuring the Incommensurable and of imagining the physiognomy of the Invisible.

The same can be said of Melville's theology. His conscious heretical choice is clear in the very name of the narrator and witness to the vision: Ishmael (in Hebrew, 'God hears'), which recalls a figure in Genesis who has an altogether special status. He is Abraham's firstborn son with the slave Hagar and he was circumcised by him, and yet, he will be not only excluded from the succession but chased into the desert with his mother. Ishmael's marginality is emphasized by Rabbinical commentaries on Genesis, which assimilate him without reason to the gentiles and even to those who will destroy the temple. This is the excluded figure whom Melville makes—together with Ahab, who in Kings renounces the God of Israel and converts

to the cult of Baal, and yet in the moment of danger remembers Yahweh—the human protagonist of his *Summa cetacea*.

Melville's theology is certainly pantheist, indeed, Spinozan (Spinoza's name, as well as Plato's, occurs a number of times in the book). Moby-Dick is not a symbol of the divinity: he is God, in the Spinozan sense in which we must say that substance is its modes—*Deus sive natura*. And among the infinite finite modes of God, Melville has chosen the greatest and most extraordinary: the white whale ('not Jove, not that great majesty Supreme! did surpass the glorified White Whale as he so divinely swam'). Only to Ahab's gnostic gaze (that he is an adept of Zoroastrian dualism is said clearly through his mysterious alter ego Fedallah, who is always called 'the Parsee') is

Moby-Dick not the figure of God, but of the evil in God, and it is because of this error that he will have to succumb, while the pantheist Ishmael will survive him.

(In the years when the photograph of the studio on Vicolo del Giglio was taken, it was not the omnipotent white whale but the pallid, exhausted copyist Bartleby who was the Melville character I was ceaselessly confronting. In any case, the apologue of the man of law and his scrivener is no less theological that *Moby-Dick*.)

You can make out the title of the book lying on the left side of the desk on Vicolo del Giglio: *La société du spectacle* by Guy Debord. I don't remember why I was rereading it—I first read it back in 1967, the very year of its publication. Guy and I became friends many years later, at the end of the eighties. I remember my first meeting with Guy and Alice at the bar of the Lutetia, the immediately intense conversation, the sure agreement about every aspect of the political situation. We had both arrived at one and the same clarity, Guy starting from the tradition of the artistic avant-gardes, myself from poetry and philosophy. For the first time I found myself speaking about politics without having to bang against the obstacle of useless and misguided ideas and writers (in a letter that Guy wrote to me some time later, one of these glibly exalted writers was soberly liquidated as 'ce sombre dément d'Althusser'[7] . . .) and the systematic exclusion of those who could have oriented the so-called movements in a less ruinous direction. In any case, it was clear to both of us that the main obstacle barring the way to a new politics was precisely what remained of the Marxist tradition (not of Marx!) and the workers' movement, which was unwittingly complicit with the enemy it believed it was combatting.

During our subsequent meetings at his house on rue du Bac, the relentless subtlety—worthy of a *magister* of Vico de li Strami or a seventeenth-century theologian—with which he analysed both capital and its two shadows, one Stalinist (the 'concentrated spectacle') and one democratic (the 'diffuse spectacle'), never ceased to amaze me.

The true problem, however, lay elsewhere—closer and, at the same time, more impenetrable. Already in one of his first films, Guy had evoked 'that clandestinity of private life regarding which we possess nothing but pitiful documents.' It was this most intimate stowaway that Guy, like the entire Western political tradition, could not get to the bottom of. And yet the term 'constructed situation', from which the group took its name, implied that it was possible to find something like 'the Northwest Passage of the geography of real life'. And if in his books and films Guy comes back so insistently to his biography, to the faces of his friends and the places where he had lived, it is because he obscurely sensed that this was exactly where the secret of politics lay hidden, the secret on which every biography and every revolution could not but run aground. The genuinely political element consists in the clandestinity of private life, and yet, if we try to grasp it, it leaves us holding only incommunicable, tedious every-dayness. It was the political significance of this stowaway—which

Aristotle had, with the name *zōē*, both included in and excluded from the city—that I had begun to investigate in those very same years. I, too, albeit in a different way, was seeking the Northwest Passage of the geography of real life.

Guy did not care at all about his contemporaries and he no longer expected anything from them. As he once told me, for him the problem of the political subject by now boiled down to the alternative between 'homme ou cave'[8] (to explain the meaning of this unknown argot term, he pointed me to a Simonin novel that he seemed fond of, *Le cave se rebiffe*). I do not know what he might have thought of the 'whatever singularity' that years later the Tiqqun group would make—with the name *Bloom*—the possible subject of the politics to come. In any case, when some years later he met the two Juliens—Coupat and Boudart—and Fulvia and Joël, I could not have imagined a closeness and, at the same time, distance greater than the one that separated them from him.

In contrast to Guy, who read narrowly but insistently (in the letter he wrote to me after reading my 'Marginal Notes on *Commentaries on the Society of the Spectacle*' he referred to the writers I had cited as 'quelques exotiques que j'ignore très regrettablement et [. . .] quatre ou cinq Français que je ne veux pas du tout lire'),[9] in the readings of Julien Coupat and his young comrades you would find the author of the *Zohar* mingling with Pierre Clastres, Marx with Jacob Frank, De Martino with René Guénon, Walter Benjamin

with Heidegger. And while Debord no longer hoped for anything from his peers—and if one despairs of others one also despairs of oneself—Tiqqun had wagered—albeit with all possible wariness—on the common man of the twentieth century, the *Bloom* as they called him, who precisely insofar as he had lost all identity and all belonging could be capable of anything, for better and for worse.

Our long discussions in the locale at 18 rue Saint-Ambroise—a cafe that they had left as it was, with its sign 'Au Vouvray', which still drew in a few passersby by mistake—and at the Verre à pied in Rue Mouffetard have remained as vivid in my memory as those that had animated the evenings at the farmhouse in Montechiarone in Tuscany ten years earlier.

In this farmhouse that Ginevra and I—following an unfathomable whim of that spirit that blows where it chooses—rented in the Sienese countryside between 1978 and 1981, we spent evenings with Peppe, Massimo, Antonella, and later, Ruggero and Maries, that I can only describe as 'unforgettable'—even if, as is the case with every truly unforgettable thing, there now remains nothing but a cloud of insignificant details, as if their truer meaning had sunk into the abyss somewhere—but the abyss, in heraldry, is the centre of the shield, and the unforgettable resembles an empty blazon. We talked about everything, a passage from Plato or Heidegger, a poem by Caproni or Penna, the colours in one of Ruggero's paintings or anecdotes from friends' lives, but as in an ancient symposium, everything found its name, its delight, and its place. All this will be lost, is already lost, entrusted to the uncertain memory of four or five people and soon to be forgotten entirely (a faint echo of it can be found in the pages of the seminar on *Language and Death*)—but the unforgettable remains, because what is lost is God's.

It was Giuseppe Russo who in these same years introduced me to Franco Nappo, whose poems were published by Quodlibet in 1996 under the title *Genere*. This collection, which passed almost unobserved, remains for me an event in Italian poetry of the later twentieth century comparable to Campana's *Canti orfici*. And the silence of the critics (with the sole—exemplary—exception of Michele Ranchetti) recalls the stupidity of the Florentine literati, whose inability to understand was betrayed by the way Campana's—evidently for them negligible—manuscript was lost. Like the broken hymn of the *Canti*, the erratic of Nappo's poetry, despite being so conspicuously visible, escaped the eyes and ears of his contemporaries, who were solely accustomed to the lower register of Montalian elegy or to postmodern mannerisms. Above all, his 'wild-eyed' lexicon, in which archaic words coexist with terms from dialect or familial jargon and a highly refined language miraculously opens the unlettered lips of the people of Forcella or San Gregorio Armeno. The effect is a unique eschatological contraction of times and languages: like the epochs, the words, too, emerge from a remote past and suddenly crash down in the present—what remains of them is something similar to the casts of the inhabitants of Pompeii, surprised and frozen forever in a gesture by the burning ashes. Theological hypostases and heroic undertakings merge lovingly with the figurines of a nativity scene and souls in purgatory walled up in their niches; Byzantine liturgies and Romanesque naves plunge into the wet lairs of the dog track in Via Domitiana or in the modest silver sign of the 'chianca 'e cavallo'.[10] At the same time there are discreet allusions and references to the poetic tradition, Virgil ('to the Gothic and Cumaean columbarium / of its great Mantuan guest') and Leopardi: 'At San Vitale Vecchio, where lay / interred the poet with his hump.' It is as if there were another language pressing from within the language, one which is neither simply dialect nor the dead language of poetry of which Pascoli spoke, but something like an Orphic lamella in which the reader can drink, like an initiate, from the 'water that comes from the lake of Mnemosyne': not language but an unassignable and immemorial memory of a language forever lost but towards which the poet stubbornly keeps travelling.

(What am I doing in this book? Am I not running the risk, as Ginevra says, of turning my studio into a little museum through which I lead readers by the hand? Do I not remain too present, while I would have liked to disappear in the faces of friends and our meetings? To be sure, for me inhabiting meant to experience these friendships and meetings with the greatest possible intensity. But instead of *inhabiting*, is it not *having* that has got the upper hand? I believe I must run this risk. There is one thing, though, that I would like to make clear: that I am an *epigone* in the literal sense of the word, a being that is generated only out of others, and that never renounces this dependency, living in a continuous, happy epigenesis.)

From the window on Vicolo del Giglio you could see only a roof and a facing wall whose plaster, deteriorated in many places, left glimpses of bricks and stones. For years my gaze must have fallen, even if only distractedly, on that piece of ochre wall burnished by time, which only I could see. What is a wall? Something that guards

and protects—the house or the city. Childlike tenderness of Italian cities, still enclosed within their own walls like a dream that stubbornly seeks shelter from reality. But a wall does not merely keep things out; it is also an obstacle that you cannot overcome, the Unsurmountable with which you must sooner or later contend. As is the case every time one comes up against a boundary, various strategies are possible. A boundary is what separates an inside from an outside. We can, then, like Simone Weil, think of a wall as such, so that it remains this way up to the end, with no hope of leaving the prison. Or rather, like Kant, we might make the boundary the essential experience, which grants us a perfectly empty outside, a sort of metaphysical storage space in which to place the inaccessible Thing in itself. Or instead, like the land surveyor K., we might question and circumvent the borders that separate the inside from the outside, the castle from the village, the sky from the earth. Or even, like the painter Apelles in the anecdote related by Pliny, cut the borderline with an even finer line in such a way that outside and inside switch sides. Make the outside inside, as Manganelli would say. In any case, the last thing to do is bang our heads against it. The last— in every sense.

I possess only one image of the studio on Piazza delle Coppelle 48, which I inherited from Giorgio Manganelli in 1967 and stayed at for three years. You can just see the wooden desk with opaque blue Formica top that I'd had made by a carpenter. The book lying on

the table is the edition in Giorgio Colli's *Encyclopedia* of Friedrich Hölderlin's *Scritti sulla poesia e frammenti*—a book that has continuously accompanied me. The French door behind me opened out onto a terrace, from which Lietta Manganelli says she witnessed the meeting between Gadda and her father when the engineer formally accused Manganelli of having written *Hilarotragoedia* as a parody of *Acquainted with Grief.*

When I met Manganelli—whose books, years later, I would never have thought of being able to do without—he had published only *Hilarotragoedia* and *La letteratura come menzogna*. I had, however, not read either. Neither had I any knowledge of the poetry of Ingeborg Bachmann, whom I met in the same years and whose poems I later tried to translate—and which I sometimes scan from memory. What held me back, what kept me from understanding? In someone like me, who cannot arrive late to an appointment, these recurring missed cues must have been a maniacal form of punctuality, as if at some level I knew I was not yet ready. Perhaps the appointment I had with their work had not yet found its hour; those two smiles, so different from each other—one almost mocking, the other shy and demanding—somehow held its announcement. Late is what fruits are called that mature slowly.

If I was not able truly to encounter them while they were alive, perhaps it is because I was afraid of them. Afraid of their exclusive and unconditional dwelling in language. Ingeborg, with the German language around her like a cloud, always waiting to be saved by her words ('O my word, save me!'), which instead always pierced and wounded her. Manganelli, happily immersed, as all visionaries are, in an uninterrupted contemplation of his language, laboriously concentrated on foiling its blackmail plot. Through language, they both saw Hell—and on that road I was not yet ready to follow them.

In Ingeborg's house on Via Bocca di Leone (the interior of which was perfectly Viennese), towards the end of the seventies, I met Gershom Scholem while he was on his way back to Jerusalem after a period of study in the Hebrew manuscript collection at the Biblioteca Palatina of Parma, the opening hours of which were so short that he was obliged to spend interminable, exhausted afternoons doing nothing in that beautiful city (about which, moreover, he said not a word). His sharp liveliness made a much greater impression on me than did the aloofness of Adorno, whom I met sometime later in the same place.

Manganelli left the small but delightful apartment in Piazza delle Coppelle (which I have dreamt of many times) because he no longer knew where to keep his books. In one of the rooms, the tiniest, which I used as a small dining room, he had stuck a series of shelving units that took up all the wall space in such a way that it was almost impossible to move. I remember how doggedly he expected me to repurchase the 'pelmet', as he called it, a horrible striped, quilted piece of fabric that he had put above the curtains of the small room that he used—and I would also use—as a studio.

I have a recurring dream where I cannot find my house in Rome, I can't exactly recall the address, the apartment is occupied by other people, and when I enter, I am not sure I recognize the three small rooms. At other times I spend a long time searching for, and failing to find, the restaurant where we used to have dinner—how can it be gone, it was right here!

These dreams retain something of the happiness and reticence of Rome in the sixties, when everything was so simple. Ginevra had rented an apartment less than five minutes away from mine, on Via Pianellari, where one evening Elvio Fachinelli brought Doctor Lacan. A few years earlier Roberto Calasso had introduced me to Joseph Rykwert, who had just published his extraordinary book on the foundational rituals of ancient cities, in which ample space was dedicated to the mundus, the circular portal that would be unsealed three times a year so that the underground world of the dead could

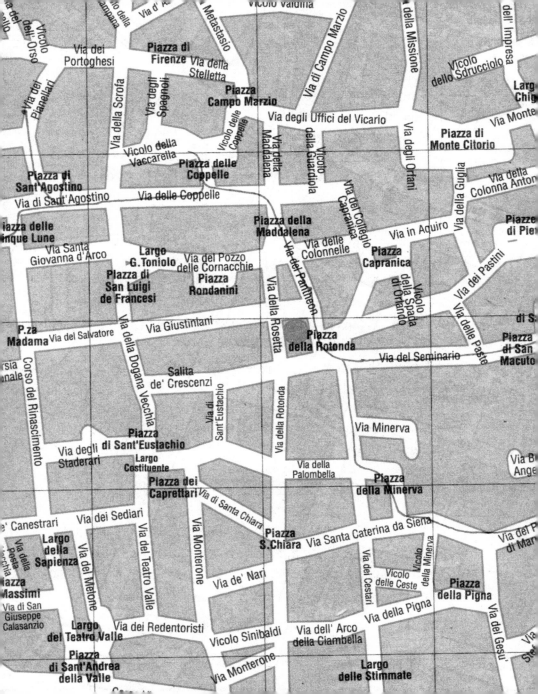

communicate with that of the living. Heidegger's Being-in-the-world and the open should be completed with this more ancient and forgotten sense of the term 'world': man does not dwell solely in the open of being, but also and above all in the gap between past and present, between the living and the dead, and it is thanks to this underground dwelling that he is able not to forget the open.

The Rome of my childhood, as if buried beneath a veil of sadness while I was discovering, in a sort of stunned astonishment, that the relations among people were not as I had thought they were. I will never forget the scene to which I owe my first clear perception of the atrocity of human injustice. As a child I was walking along a street—perhaps in the Flaminio neighbourhood, where I lived—and I suddenly saw a door open and a middle-aged man being pushed and kicked out of it. I remember perfectly that as he was getting up and picking his glasses up off the ground and putting them back on, he repeatedly sobbed 'I am the accountant Ghislanzoni, I am the accountant Ghislanzoni . . . ' From that moment the idea of injustice entered my mind and heart and has never left.

In the bookcase on Piazza delle Coppelle, which you can't see in the photograph, I kept in view the Plon edition of the *Cahiers* of Simone Weil, which I had bought in Paris in 1964 at the Tschann bookstore on Boulevard du Montparnasse, which I frequented intensely. When I returned to Rome, I gave them to Elsa to read, and she was dazzled—as was I, so much so that I decided to dedicate my thesis in philosophy of law to Simone Weil's thought.

With the passage of time, the description of her thought as 'mystical'—a term to be used with care, which often serves to exclude and marginalize a work that can't be classified—seems increasingly inadequate to me. Are those so very precise and peremptory analyses of the European political situation in the 1930s 'mystical'? And the articles on Germany on the threshold of Nazism? The critique of the ruin of social democracy and of political parties? Is the meticulous, detailed critique of classical and post-quantum science that she carried out in a series of essays in 1941 mystical (the densest of which begins with this surprising diagnosis: 'Il s'est passé pour nous, gens d'Occident, une chose bien étrange au tournant de ce siècle; nous avons perdu la science sans nous en apercevoir . . . ')?[11] And the distinction between inert truths, which are deposited in the memory without acting in any way and that we thus believe we possess (this is the knowledge that is taught in universities and schools, of which Simone Weil says that 'to have a great deal of inert truth in the mind is of little use'),[12] and active truths, whose presence unburdens the soul of errors and pushes it in the search for the good—might this not belong to the purest philosophy?

It does not surprise me that one of her most attentive readers was an Epicurean, Jean Fallot, who saw an analogy between the experience of *malheur*—so central for Simone Weil—and pleasure in Epicurus. Epicurus thinks of what happens in the soul when pain ceases. Weil does the exact opposite: she thinks of what happens in a person when all pleasure vanishes, the instant in which we feel emptied of all energy and all resources and we perceive our life 'as a mere fact in which there is no good whatsoever'.[13] This is certainly a frightful thing, but it is also the truth that we must not cease to contemplate if we want to reach the good in its purest form.

In any case, at that time what particularly struck me was the critique of the notions of the person and of law developed in 'Human Personality'. It was starting with this critique that I read Mauss' essay on the notion of the *persona*, and the nexus that intimately joined the juridical person and the theatrical—and then theological—mask of the modern individual seemed clear to me. Perhaps the critique of law that I have never abandoned since the first volume of *Homo Sacer* has its earliest roots in Weil's essay.

I still possess the worn and creased copy of the book containing that essay, *Écrits de Londres et dernières lettres*, published by Gallimard in 1957 as part of the 'Espoir' series edited by Albert Camus. Oddly, for reasons I can no longer recall, the book is marked and annotated in pen by José Bergamín, as if the copy had belonged to him.

Simone Weil, who so clearly sees the inadequacy of the notions of law and the person and their conjunction in the 'rights of man', unwittingly falls back into the law when she seeks to substitute them with symmetrically opposite concepts such as 'obligation', 'consensus', and 'punishment'. A 'Déclaration des obligations' is nothing but the flip side of the 'Déclaration des droits'.

The problem of seeing the limitations of a writer whom one loves was stated by Coleridge (regarding the difficulty of reading Plato) in the form of a hermeneutic principle that I have tried to follow as far as possible: 'Until you understand a writer's ignorance, presume yourself ignorant of his understanding.' With a slight variation, this can be reformulated thus: 'If you believe you have understood what a writer has understood, do not therefore presume to have understood what he has not understood.'

When we think we have perceived a writer's limits or incoherencies, it is well to doubt our understanding of his ignorance. This is why, rather than decrying presumed contradictions, I prefer to seek what remains unsaid behind them and to comprehend and develop it. In this case, it seems to me, that is the idea of the impersonal: 'So far from its being his person, what is sacred in a human being is the impersonal in him. [. . .] Perfection is impersonal. Our personality is the part of us which belongs to error and sin.'[14] What is impersonal in a being cannot have anything to do with rights or obligations, and even less can it 'consent' or 'be punished'. And this impersonal element is what corresponds to the joy that in the last fragments written in London she forcefully opposes to *malheur*: 'Joy is an essential need of the soul. The lack of joy, whether it be a matter of *malheur* or simply boredom, is a state of illness in which intelligence, courage, and generosity are extinguished. It is an asphyxia. Human thought is nourished by joy.' And again: 'All that I wish for exists, or has existed, or will exist somewhere. For I am incapable of complete invention. In that case, how should I not be satisfied?'[15]

Weil: only human beings who have fallen into the most extreme state of social degradation can tell the truth; everyone else lies.

One can speak the truth only on the condition that no one is listening (the truth is that which, upon hearing it, you cannot believe). A truth pronounced by an authoritative mouth that already has its assured listeners loses something of its truth. This is why we seek in writing to become anonymous, to make ourselves unknown, even to ourselves. Only a truth that is lost can be unexpectedly, obliquely picked up. Hence the vanity of all institutions entrusted with the task of transmitting the truth.

And this, I believe, is why I have never been able, nor wanted, to have students, but only friends, even when differences of age were so great that friendship was difficult. And of all those whom I could see as teachers, none ever intentionally assumed that posture. On the contrary, all of them—Pepe, Giovanni, even Heidegger during the seminars at Le Thor—were uniquely hesitant to present themselves as teachers, and always found a way to refuse such trappings.

In the bookcase to the right in the studio on Vicolo del Giglio, you can see a photo of José Bergamín, who, along with Giovanni, certainly made a mark on my youth. In a certain sense, Pepe was the opposite of Simone Weil. Every meeting with him happened under the sign of joy, and of joy so different and intense each time that we would return home incredulous, transfigured and buoyant, as if a joy like this could not exist or be borne. And yet, in my—or his—copy of *Écrits de Londres*, Pepe annotated a number of passages where we find the word *malheur*, something with which his life as an exile and subject of political persecution must have made him familiar. But the passage on joy is marked with his unmistakable signature in the form of a bird.

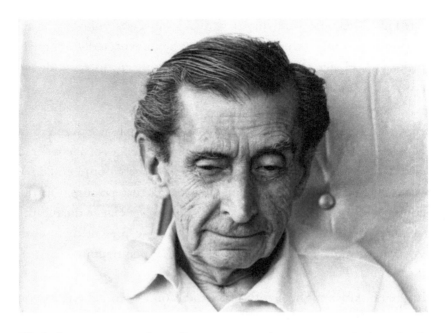

He is the person to whom I owe my aversion to every tragic attitude and my inclination towards comedy—even though I later came to understand that philosophy was beyond or before tragedy and comedy, and that, as Socrates suggests at the end of the *Symposium*, anyone who knows how to write tragedies must also know how to write comedies. And it is also thanks to Pepe that I understood early on that God is not a monopoly of priests and that, like salvation, I could search for God only *extra Ecclesiam*. When Elsa told me that she wanted to write a book titled *Without the Comforts of Religion*, I immediately felt that this title spoke to me, that, like Pepe, I lived in

pouvoir faire. Je n'ai pas de spécialité, de qualifications techniques particulières; je n'ai rien en dehors de la culture générale qui nous est commune, excepté (si cela peut être utilisé) une certaine expérience des milieux populaires acquise par contact personnel. J'ai été un an ouvrière sur machines dans diverses usines de la région parisienne, dont Renault, en 1934-35; j'avais pris un an de congé pour cela. J'ai encore les certificats. L'été dernier, j'ai travaillé dans les champs, notamment six semaines comme vendangeuse dans un village du Gard.

Toute tâche n'exigeant pas de connaissances techniques et comportant un degré élevé d'efficacité, de peine et de danger me conviendrait parfaitement.

La peine et le péril sont indispensables à cause de ma conformation mentale. Il est heureux que tous ne l'aient pas, sans quoi toute action organisée serait impossible, mais moi, je ne puis pas la changer; je le sais par une longue expérience. Le malheur répandu sur la surface du globe terrestre m'obsède et m'accable au point d'annuler mes facultés, et je ne puis les récupérer et me délivrer de cette obsession que si j'ai moi-même une large part de danger et de souffrance. C'est donc une condition pour que j'aie la capacité de travailler.

Je vous supplie de me procurer, si vous pouvez, la quantité de souffrance et de danger utiles qui me préservera d'être stérilement consumée par le chagrin. Je ne peux pas vivre dans la situation où je me trouve en ce moment. Cela me met tout près du désespoir.

Je ne peux pas croire qu'on ne puisse pas me procurer cela. L'afflux des demandes ne doit pas être tel, pour les tâches dangereuses et pénibles, qu'il n'y ait pas une place disponible. Et même s'il n'y en a pas, il est facile d'en créer. Car il y a beaucoup, beaucoup à faire, vous le savez comme moi.

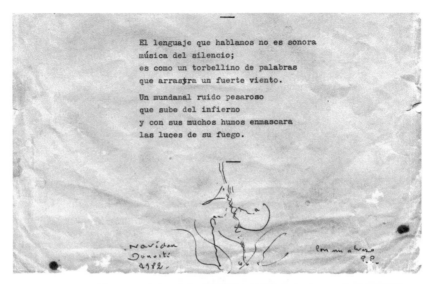

El lenguaje que hablamos no es sonora
música del silencio;
es como un torbellino de palabras
que arrastra un fuerte viento.

Un mundanal ruido pesaroso
que sube del infierno
y con sus muchos humos enmascara
las luces de su fuego.

some way with God but without the comforts of religion. (This also allowed me to escape those people—and there were many in Italy—who wanted to convince me that *extra Partitum nulla salus*.)

Extra: outside (with the idea of a movement starting from inside—*ex*—the idea of an exit). It is not possible to find the truth if one does not first exit from the situation—or institution—that impedes access. The philosopher must become a stranger in his own city; Illich had to somehow leave the church and Simone Weil could never decide to enter it. *Extra* is the place of thought.

Rome, 13 July 2014: 'Tonight's dream. I was with Pepe and some other people in the house where he lived in Spain. It was a very simple and wonderful house, like all the houses where I met him: a large room that opened out onto two connected terraces, just as large. There was little furniture, all of it of wood, among which I noticed a small chair that I brought closer to Pepe so he could sit, but instead he put his feet on it. Then we went out in a car to continue the evening, perhaps to go to dinner but probably without aim. We were happy. Every moment of the dream was so full of joy that I somehow almost consciously delayed its end, as if joy were the material out of which the dream was made and nothing must stop my mind from weaving. In the end, waking up, I realized that the joy the dream was made of was none other than Pepe.'

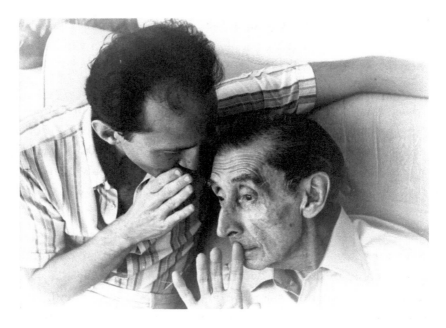

It is through Pepe that I discovered Spain—Pepe, of all people, who had passed a good part of his life in exile. His Madrid, to be sure, so modest and grey in the neighbourhood of the old mosque—and then Seville and Andalusia, blinded by sun. But before that, the last traces of something like a people, the pueblo-village that for him was not a substance but always and only a *minoría*: not a numerical portion but rather that which prevents a people from coinciding with itself, from being everything. And this was the only concept of a people that could interest me.

I remember him saying to me one day that he had realized the Spanish people had died before him and that this was the most tragic moment of his entire life. To survive one's own people—this is our condition, but it is perhaps also the extreme poetic condition.

His three fundamental reading experiences: Spinoza (at 16 years old), Pascal and Nietzsche. When I pointed out to him that his formative writers included no Spaniards, he answered: 'But this is Spain exactly!'

He would say that the distance of God is the intimacy of life. That the aesthete refuses repetition, the pharisee repeats without enthusiasm. But to repeat with enthusiasm, that is man.

He would say that the essential thing about the verónica is the right moment: the toreador must wait for the moment when the bull's head is taken in the muleta (like the face of Christ leaving its image in the woman's veil). If he waits a second more or less it is lost.

Pepe's buoyancy—his legendary frivolity—lay entirely in the volatile and insubstantial quality of his 'I'. He was perfectly himself because he never *was* himself. He was like a breeze or a cloud or a smile—absolutely present but never constrained to an identity (this is why the condition of official nonexistence that the Spanish government forced upon him by depriving him of his documents suited and amused him). His entire doctrine of the *I* is summarized in a verse by Lope that he liked to recite—'Yo me sucedo a mi mismo [I am my own successor].' The I is nothing other than this succeeding of oneself, 'entering oneself' [*insearsi*] and 'exiting oneself' [*infuorarsi*]— or infuriation [*infuriarsi*]—as he would say, ceaselessly going out of oneself and coming back into oneself, losing oneself and grasping oneself—ultimately only 'un punto de la nada en que todo se cruza', an empty point in which everything intersects, following, as he wrote of his beloved Lope, 'the dictation of the air that sketches it.' Airy— this is what Pepe was: this is why he loved to sign his name in the form of a bird.

On the snow that untouched
disguises the landscape
three drops of blood
wondrously.

Without closing the eyes
near and far
a shudder of wings
invisibly.

There is a photograph of Pepe standing on the side of a road holding a bag, as if he were waiting for a bus—but he seems to shudder with impatience as he waits. His joy was like this—an impatient joy, perhaps because it was a Christian joy, necessarily waiting. That is how I remember him in his last years, when he was awaiting death—the 'hand of snow'—with a sort of impatient fervour. Just like Pepe's, my waiting, too, is sustained by hope and hurry.

An Islamic legend says that because of impatience Adam sought to gather the forbidden fruits of the tree even before he was able to stand on his feet. 'Then the spirit moved though Adam's body until it reached his legs. And Adam became flesh, blood, bones, veins, nerves and bowels, except his feet, which remained clay. He tried to stand but was unable, which is the meaning of His Words: *Man was created of haste.*'[16]

Impatience is the reason we write; impatience is the reason we stop writing. But the fruits—impatience prevents us from gathering them. And this is good. Patience is perhaps a virtue—but only impatience is holy. An impatience that becomes method. Style, like asceticism, is the fruit of a restrained impatience.

Giovanni and Pepe never actually crossed paths in my life, and yet a persistent counterpoint binds them together in a fugue with no answer. Theirs were two different kinds of fragility: one marked by an invisible but deep crack, the other intact and without secrets, like a shining and most delicate porcelain. The one seemed unbreakable because he was, in truth, already broken; the other always on the verge of going to pieces but, in truth, impossible to chip.

My first encounter with Spain had occurred many years earlier, in 1961, when I met a group of artists who were staying at the Accademia di Spagna in Piazza di San Pietro in Montorio. I became closest to two of them, the sculptor Francisco (Paco) López and his wife Isabel Quintanilla, a painter. It was as if the damage that surrounded them and that they somehow accepted could not contaminate them. I remember how Paco, while modelling the creased sheets of a little clay bed with a sleeping figure, almost ecstatically sounded out the word *realidad*, which had been passed on to him as a mantra by his friend and teacher Antonio López. I only recently learned that Paco and Isabel, together with other painters perhaps inaccurately classified as 'realists', had a show dedicated to them at the Thyssen-Bornemisza Museum in Madrid.

The *Granadas* and the *Cuarto de baño* painted by Isabel a few years after our meeting fill me with joy, and in Paco's *Bodegón con membrillos* I find once again the wonderful attention to the quotidian that had moved me then. Through these works our destinies return delicately, imperiously to brush against one another after half a century. When I met them, Paco and Isabel, along with Antonio López, María Moreno, Julio López and Carmen Laffon, were reconstructing in Spain the language of figurative painting, which seemed lost. 'We were,' Antonio López said ironically, 'like people who returned again after a long time to make a new painting, a new history.' To return again to something after a long time: in the same years in Italy, Ruggero Savinio was travelling back and forth along his 'paths of the figure'. But while the figures on his canvases contain and show all the tracks along his path through time, in Isabel, Antonio and Paco those tracks seem erased: but if one looks and listens more carefully, here, too, we can see the figure re-emerging intact after a long pilgrimage through time, originating in the immemorial and shining motionless for a moment before setting out again.

Though I lived there for nearly eight years, I do not have a single image of my first studio in Venice, whose windows opened onto Campo Santa Barbara. But during a visit to Venice in June 1996, Mario Dondero took a picture of me in the large living room next to the studio. On the wall above me you can see one of the sheets sewn and painted by Clio Pizzingrilli, which accompanied me in those

happy years and which I thought of as something like the banners of a coming people. In that house Martina, Francesca and Valeria lived with me, as well as, in long and impassioned evenings, my dearest friends: Andrea, Daniel, Emanuele and, until the falling out that separated us for good, Guido. It is there that the *Homo Sacer* project started to take shape and where the book about Auschwitz, *The Time That Remains* (which Yan Thomas thought was my best book), and *The Open* were written. And it is from that building—which was the old Casin de' Nobili, where the Venetians received foreigners—that I, a stranger in turn, came to know Venice intimately, came to discover that a dead city can, like a ghost, be secretly more alive than not only its inhabitants but nearly all the cities that I have known.

Yan Thomas, the most brilliant historian of Roman law that I ever met, also loved Venice. And it was in Venice that we once improvised a small three-person seminar on monastic rules—a theme on which my studies intersected with his last projects, which death prevented him from completing. Like me, Yan distrusted the law's attempts to join itself to life, to immediately transform the living being into a juridical subject, and yet, he could not help but admire the artifices and fictions through which Roman law had responded to this task. Modern law's tendency towards a growing and immediate juridification of life deeply repelled him, and this is where the archaeology of law that I had begun with *Homo Sacer* intersected with his concerns.

In Paris we would meet for breakfast at the old Polidor restaurant in rue Monsieur le Prince, where for a few years I rented a small apartment that had been left to me by Toni Negri. When I received the news of Yan's death in September 2008, it seemed to me like the very ground I walked on had vanished, the ground I was by then so used to sharing with him.

After having to leave the studio on Vicolo del Giglio and before moving to Venice, I lived for a few years in Rome in the house on Via Corsini at the Botanical Garden where I had lived with Ginevra and where I still live from time to time. Here, on the same desk, there is now an engraving that depicts *Cupid Riding a Snail*, which might be the most beautiful example of *festina lente* that I have ever come across—and it is especially meaningful to the impatient person that I am. In some ways it is my heraldic badge, my motto in an image: restrained impatience. This is why I reproduced it as the frontispiece of the second edition of *Idea of Prose*, as if it contained the idea of this work in which I see myself more than in others, perhaps because in this work I was able to forget myself (Karen Blixen said that mottoes are the most important thing in life, certainly more effective than any psychoanalysis.)

Next to this, in the letter tray, there is a photograph of one of Titian's last paintings, *The Flaying of Marsyas*, which is held in the gallery of Kroměříž Castle. For years I have continuously mediated on this

painting in which Titian depicted himself in the figure of Midas, who compassionately watches the torture of the satyr. And I cannot help but associate it with Dante's invocation at the beginning of the *Paradise*, which sees being ripped out of one's own skin as an image of inspiration:

> come into my breast and breath there, as when you
> drew Marsyas forth from the sheath of his members.[17]

So arduous is the task of the poet—being skinned alive in order to sing.

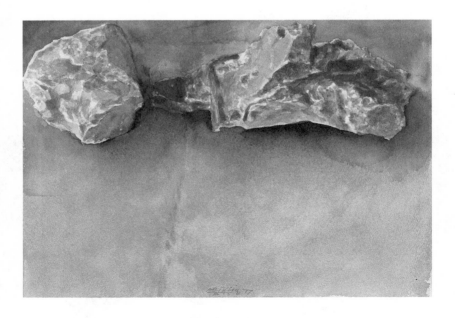

Why has painting been—and ever increasingly is—an essential part of my life? In the eighties, I shared in Ruggero Savinio's impassioned research almost every day; later, thanks to Monica, I discovered the incomparable work of Avigdor Arikha. In the same years the painters of Scicli, especially Sonia Alvarez and Piero Guccione, had helped me not to lose my sense of sight, which our times try everything possible to blind (in my studio in Vetralla there is a watercolour by Avigdor and a seascape in the form of a bedspread by Sonia). And I just recently rediscovered Isabel Quintanilla, Paco and Antonio López . . .

As Monica never gets tired of saying, painting—even the most realistic—always flows into myth. For me, painting truly is silent poetry, speech rendered silent in an image—but for this very reason exposed as speech, as *muthos*. That there is speech and its silence is seen—and in this silence the thing appears for a moment restored to its anonymity, to its not yet or no longer having a name.

On the right-hand side of the desk in Vicolo del Giglio you can see eight similar notebooks bound in different colours. They are notebooks in which I write down thoughts, observations, reading notes, citations—on rare occasions dreams, meetings or particular events. They are an essential part of my research laboratory and they often contain the first germ or the materials of a future book or one that I am in the process of writing. Begun in December 1979, they now number thirty and in my studio in Venice they thus take up a full row in the bookshelf. I realize that I have given a description of their exterior and that I would not know how to describe what these notebooks really are, that at times they seem to me to be the most living and precious part of my life and at other times to be inert dross. To be sure, compared to my finished books, these notebooks, with their hurried and ragged handwriting, are a more faithful image of potentiality, which keeps intact the possibility to be and not to be, or to be otherwise. In this sense, these notebooks are my studio. This is why I prefer them to my published books and at times wish I had not carried them across the threshold towards final publication. I have many times thought about writing a book that was only the proem or postlude of a missing book. Perhaps the books that I have published are something of this sort—not books but preludes or epilogues. A writer's secret lies entirely in the blank space that separates the notebooks from the book.

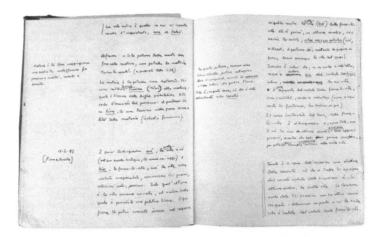

Notebooks as a form of study and study as essentially unfinished. The 'form of the research' and the 'form of the exposition', notes and draft are not opposed to one another: in a certain sense the finished work is also itself a fragment and research project. As in music, every ricercar ends in a fugue, but the fugue is literally endless.

On the far right-hand side of my desk in Venice stands a photograph by Salgado showing the face of a girl. Her name is unknown to me, but I know with certainty that she will be the one to judge me on the last day, to condemn me, as her severe and pained expression seems to suggest, or to absolve me. She is the image of the *daena* in Iranian soteriology, who will come to meet us on the *novissima dies* and whose features we ourselves have formed with our actions and thoughts.

Next to her you can see a poem by Giorgio Caproni, the one that begins 'I retuned there / where I had never been', which he had copied for me in 1982—giving me, as well, the tormented original manuscript, dated 31 January 1971, 'one of the very few,' he wrote in the letter that accompanied it, 'that was saved by chance from my usual (and hygienic) destruction.' The poem also appears on the dresser in the studio on Vicolo del Giglio, right under the two prints by Redon. Among the poets whom I have met, Caproni is the one I have most admired—that is, regarded in every instant with absolute wonder. Wonder in the face of an apparently simple and retiring man who had put into poetry—and thus lived, if life is what springs from the word and remains inseparable from it—unprecedented experiences, like an animal that a mutation had brought beyond the confines of its own species but which is impossible to place in any other *phulon*.

Here there is no sense in trying to decide between what is poetry and what is life: the impossible meeting with the unmarried mother in the *Versi livornesi* certainly happened in the biography of the poet, just as the shattering of the wonderful weaving of Caproni's metre is indistinguishable from the undoing of Italian society that began at the end of the seventies.

No less evident in Caproni is the intimacy of thought and poetry. I remember how, while I was working on the editing of the seminar *Language and Death*, I was struck precisely by the poem 'Return' in *The Wall of the Earth*. Having-been, which in Hegel and again in Heidegger marks the outer edge, the abyss of Western thought, is here leaped over towards a figure of being—the never-was—that is truly anarchic and beyond time, with neither origin nor end, neither past nor future. And this never-was, with its half-filled glass 'on the chequered / oilcloth', is this poet's habitual dwelling place, where 'everything / still remains just as / I never left it'.

A Giorgio Agamben,
1975 Corsini, 29/3/82

31/1/78

In our conversations, Caproni compared the broken prosody of *Il Conte di Kevenhüller* to a recitative, a sort of counter-song that runs through the words like an agitated ritardando without ever coinciding with them. As for the ellipsis marks that are so characteristic of the late books, he would say that they were suggested to him by the adagio of Schubert's String Quintet op. 163, in which the pizzicato always comes in to interrupt the melodic phrase that the violin is never able to carry to completion. It is as if thought were halting any headway made by the song and the song tenaciously started up again precisely thanks to the cadence that had stopped it. Thought and poetry are the two intensities, both from the muses, that cross and animate the single field of language.

This is perhaps why the final end of art and the furthest edge of poetry cannot be anything but a point of desistance, the point where thought can keep up with and adhere to the beauty it follows only by letting go:

> but now my following after her beauty in
> poetry must desist, as must every artist at his
> ultimate limit.[18]

A recurring dream that Caproni related to me in various versions. He and a friend take the tram to visit a place he knows very well, 'I go there often, a daily walk almost.' At a certain point he looks at his watch and sees that it is time to go back. But when he looks for the terminus of the usual tram, he can't find it, and if he asks someone, the answer is: ' "The terminus? The tram? But here, dear sir, there have never been trams." I ask someone else, same response. I start to get frightened and search around at random. I get more and more lost. I end up in a rural area, far outside the city. Every way back completely lost. I wake up.'

Every way back lost: anywhere he goes, it is as if Caproni had reached a point of no return, *ad portam inferi*, like Anna Picchi at the station in the poem of that title in *Il seme del piangere*, or as in the countless pages of the unfinished and tortured manuscript of a poem that begins 'Ego qui ad portas veni inferi et vidi . . . '[19]

'I / have arrived at a quiet / despair, undaunted' reads the confession that concludes the ceremonious traveller's farewell. But already in the astonishing verses of the *Third Book*, the metric tension of the 'accumulated enjambments' restores, like a breathless panting, the 'pallid and headlong despair' of the decade between 1944 and 1954. Here the style is extremely elevated, and yet the poems are shot through with everyday terms—car headlights, bicycles, slippers, cafes, trams, elevators (Caproni once admitted that he was suspicious of any poem in which a bicycle did not appear).

Proudly defending the elevated style, Adam Zagajewski has rightly observed that in European culture there seems to be a prevalent and mistaken conviction that the use of the high register in poetry is something reactionary. Instead, the high style can coexist not only with humour but also with a modest vocabulary: the tone of a poem does not depend on the vocabulary but on the tension that springs directly from the voice of the muse—from Calliope or Erato, Melpomene or Urania (and even Thalia, the muse of comedy, can touch upon the sublime). In Italian literature from the twentieth century to today, what had rightly begun as a resistance to D'Annunzio's rhetorical style ended up producing a flattening down to the lowest style, which has erased every trace of music and thought from the language. But a language that has severed all ties to its origination in the muses and has lost even the memory of them is no longer a language.

It was Caproni who put me in touch with his beloved Carlo Betocchi, whom I went to visit with Ginevra in April of 1984 in the rest home in Fiesole where he spent the last years of his life. The nun who answered the door told us that he was probably in the garden and that she would tell him we were there. And it is there that he met us, cheerful, dressed in grey with a large blue tie, asking 'Who is looking for me?', his face brightening immediately upon hearing that Caproni had sent us. He spoke of his favourite poets, Dino Campana and Rimbaud, and of Clemente Rebora, whom he had met for the first time on his death bed. As a 'man with a job' who for many years worked as a land surveyor and foreman in Rome, Tuscany and Frosinone, Betocchi contrasted himself to the Florentine litterateurs who 'lived from their work'. Before coming out to lunch with us he brought us up to his room, a simple little bedroom with a cot, but with a light-filled balcony that opened out onto a marvellous vision of the city. On one shelf were all his books, which he had had brought to him because he could no longer remember their titles. *Il sale del canto, Un passo, un altro passo, L'estate di San Martino, Poesie del sabato, Del sempre* . . . like Caproni's, these books I cannot forget.

' . . . this thing that rises up as both a profound anguish and joy is the salt of the song; it is the first flavour that one tastes of the song. It is the substance of the song, the land of possible new revolution, while that which we have called contentment calls out from below [. . .]. Where it breaks off is peace. I would like to add: when it is truly a song it breaks off before—a moment before—the poem; it lets the heart beat for a moment more, humanly alone.'[20]

> Come, come to me, now that I am old,
> love no, but you shadow of love made
> of mute everyday things, views
> of rooftops and streets, of opened windows
> from which lovers watch the approach

of their lover, or sickly women behind glass panes,
And the haggard procession of pitiful
days, and your shadowy peace lost
as the drowning coot, blasted in flight,
a few feathers still floating in the air,
is lost in the marsh:
I am the reality that staggers here
without even a reason why
if you do not come, love, shadow of love,
or sweet sleep, to give me your rest.[21]

On the wall above my desk in Venice, you can see a postcard from Alfred Jarry, which I bought from an antique dealer in Paris along with a ticket for the first performance of *Ubu roi* on 11 December 1896, at the Théâtre de l'Œuvre. My encounter with Jarry had been an early one, and I had already in 1967 translated *The Supermale* for the series 'Il Pesanervi', which I then edited with Ginevra. And a few years before that, *Doctor Faustroll* had dazzled me as the most rigorous attempt to come to terms poetically with a genuinely philosophical problem. Here, with incredible self-confidence, Jarry puts

Bergson's courses at the Lycée Henri-IV—which he had attended and meticulously recorded in the notebooks now kept at the Doucet Library—to good use. If pataphysics is a joke, it is only so in the sense that Plato in the *Sixth Letter* defines playfulness as the 'sister of solemnity':[22] it truly is what is added to metaphysics and moves beyond it towards a further universe.

Anyone who hopes to write philosophy without either explicitly or implicitly taking on the poetic problem of its form is not a philosopher. This must have been what Wittgenstein had in mind when he wrote 'philosophy ought really to be written only as a *poetic composition*.'[23] This, in any case, is how it has always been for me: I became a philosopher in order to deal with a poetic aporia that I could not get to the bottom of. In this sense, I am perhaps not a philosopher but a poet, just as, conversely, many works that are thought to be literary instead rightfully belong to philosophy. Jarry's work is certainly among the latter. He constructs a poetic machine in order to define in the most apt way what he unequivocally calls the Absolute. Not, as he immediately clarifies, 'the deadly and metaphysical Absolute' that is based on 'Being or Saying' (that is, onto-logy) but the 'dynamic Absolute', which is based on Life (that is, 'ontogeny'). One of his most philosophically dense texts is the description of a machine that allows one to step out of the flow of time in order to stand immobile in time and thereby explore it. The machine is described in extremely convincing scientific terms, but it is clear that the machine is one and the same with the book that the author is writing. Every book that Jarry wrote is, in this sense, a poetic solution to a philosophical problem.

If *Dr Faustroll* (including 'How to Construct a Time Machine') and 'Being and Living' are Jarry's metaphysics, his ethics is entirely contained in *Ubu roi*. Jarry lived this ethics, which is no less scandalous than that of the cynics, with a rigor and immediacy that never ceased to astound his friends. He had transformed farce into an ascetic practice so total and demanding that he disappeared into it completely. The mask—le père Ubu—devoured its creator—nothing remained of him. The use of 'we'—or, at times, the third person—instead of 'I', the impassive fixity of the facial features, the hammering, nasal voice that so annoyed Rachilde (*Ma-da-me*), the absolute indifference to his own existence and to social convention—all of this is cynically and peremptorily pushed all the way to holiness. He was able to realize in his own person what Kleist had only dared to dream of: the total and beatific transfiguration of man into a marionette.

In the same years that I was discovering Jarry, I bought the first edition of René Crevel's *Êtes-vous-fous* from a bouquiniste along the Seine. I have tried various times to translate it, as I do with the books I love written in a foreign language, but in this case the language was so foreign it seemed untranslatable to me. And not only was the book untranslatable, its untranslatability was inseparable from an equally perfect illegibility. I realize that I could say the same about Melville's and Jarry's books, and that some of the books I love best are literally illegible to me. Or that they must be read in a totally different way, perceiving not the meaning and the discourse, but the

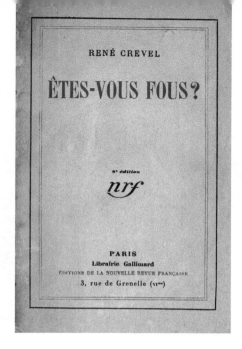

language—that language!—as in Caproni's *Anniversary Sonnets*, whose syllables I sound out ecstatically without understanding them. One must spend hours on a single page without even dreaming of reading the next, and then repeat the experience with another page, staying there even longer. Here, too, as with the time machine invented by Faustroll, the time of reading stops 'in a standstill between past and future which should be called the *imaginary present*', where succession is reversed into regression and what takes place is not a progressive reading but the becoming of a memory. One does not read the book: one spells it out through a series of separate and unforgettable memories that emerge from an immemorable point outside of time.

This is how I have read and reread the books I love best.

emmène l'oiseau-flamme, pour qu'il se repose, au plus haut étage d'un sanatorium gratte-ciel. — Le rucher à malades. — L'heure des gramophones. — Pour échapper au naufrage, à l'aube montagnarde, le regard s'accrochait au fer du balcon. — Privé même d'un tel secours, aujourd'hui, rue des Paupières-Rouges, en plein brouillard, l'homme devient, pour de vrai, M. Vagualame. — Yolande en chair et en os, très décolletée malgré le froid, jaillit du trottoir de brume. — Suivent Mimi Patata et les jumeaux. — Yolande emmène tout ce monde chez elle.

La Ville.

Elle porte collier de visages en papier mâché, mais son chignon joue à l'arc de triomphe.

Ainsi, avant l'ère des nuques rases, toute patronne de bistrot, à coups de guiches, frisettes, franges, boucles, nattes, compliquait, en de chimériques architectures, l'édifice de cheveux et d'orgueil, à même le sol du crâne.

Or la dernière auvergnate, penchée sur le zinc d'un comptoir, où se mire sa tignasse bouffie de crêpés cimentée à la brillantine, étayée de peignes et barrettes, façon écaille, nymphe de gargote, narcisse femelle, mais défiant tout vertigo — elle vous en donne sa parole — car la tête est bonne, certes, meilleure

For a few years now, on the wall of my Venice studio next to the Jarry manuscript, there has been a small drawing by Bonnard, probably a sketch for one of the *nus à la baignoire*. I first saw Bonnard's painting in Paris in 1967, in the first large retrospective at the Musée de l'Orangerie, and since then I have never grown tired of looking at it. If, according to the meaning of the Hebrew term, the 'Nabi' painters are prophets, then Bonnard's prophecy has to do with colour. With an intentional inversion of the traditional relation between the two terms, a passage in his notebooks reads: 'Drawing is sensation, colour is reason.' Intelligence—the intellect of love—that turns itself into chromaticism, the ecstasy of intelligence in colour: This is Bonnard— supreme knowledge. My idea of happiness is entirely saturated with his light.

A chapter of *Dr Faustroll* is dedicated to Pierre Bonnard. And Jarry's *Ubu* is inseparable from the *Ubu* of Bonnard, who signed the lively vignettes of the 1899 *Almanach* as well as the series of croquis for Vollard's pamphlets about Ubu. But it is as if Jarry's ferocious and childlike ink had been transfigured in Bonnard's colours into paradisiacal ardour.

The enigma of Marthe's body, which appears countless times on canvases and in photographs, depicted with meticulous delight—but her face always fades into the shadow. It is the only omen of death in Bonnard's Arcadia.

If I think about what Paris and France has meant to me, I cannot help but recall my meeting and friendship, around the mid-sixties, with Pierre Klossowski, and exactly 20 years later, with Jean-Luc Nancy. I had read Pierre's *Such a Deathly Desire* and *The Suspended Vocation* in something like frenzy and, for once, the writer seemed no less extraordinary than his books—he was perhaps the only person, as I was to learn later, who dared to push himself to the extreme in the direction indicated by Fourier.

As for Jean-Luc (who, unlike Pierre, was my age), for years, in our frequent meetings in Strasbourg or in Italy, I felt him to be so close to my thought that sometimes it seemed to me like our voices became one. And it is on the question of the voice that our reflections first intersected. My copy of *Partage des voix* is filled with marginal notes,[24] and my short text on *The End of Thought* made such an impression on him that in the prosopopoeias of 'Vox clamans in deserto' he puts me on stage—along with Valéry, Rousseau, and Hegel—to recite some lines. Since then, I have not ceased to reflect on the voice and I believe that if thought and poetry converge towards a common vanishing point, this point cannot be anything but the voice. Beginning in the nineties, for reasons that need not be

examined here, Jean-Luc began to distance himself further and further away from my work—but friendship, which is the immediate sharing of the sensation of existing, reignites for me equally every time I return to visit him.

Benjamin is present in every studio where I have worked: in a manuscript letter on the dresser on Vicolo del Giglio, right next to the poem by Caproni; in a photograph taken in Ibiza given to me by Jean Selz; and in the transcription of a dream in my studio in Venice.

Even if I could never have met him, among my teachers he is the one whom I feel I have most often run into in person. When you become materially—that is, philologically—intimate with a writer's work, when reading his books makes your hands shake, you experience phenomena that seem magical, but in truth are only the fruit of that intimacy. It thus happens that upon opening a book you find the passage you were looking for, or you immediately find the answer to or the perfect formulation of a troubling question—or, as happened to me with Benjamin, you end up physically running into things and people that he had seen and touched.

I recall my emotion when in January 1977 I discovered in a phone book that Herbert Blumenthal Belmore, who had spent a great deal of time with Benjamin in the years of the German Youth Movement, lived a little more than 100 meters from my studio on Vicolo del Giglio. It was in his apartment on Via Sora, where I often went to visit him, that my first material encounter with Benjamin occurred: and it occurred, unexpectedly, because of the vehemence of Blumenthal's hatred for his sometime friend—or rather, his rejected love which had turned into rancour. Benjamin had suddenly broken off their friendship in 1917 (they had become friends in 1910), and at more than 60 years' distance Blumenthal's bitterness was so relentless that he even arrived at saying venomously that Benjamin had met the end he deserved. And yet, the love that fed this hatred must have been just as ardent, since he had carefully saved not only his friend's letters but also some unpublished manuscripts and—

something that moved me in particular—a little blue notebook in which Carla Seligson had, in a clear cursive calligraphy, copied the poems of Fritz Heinle that had been lost in 1933 during Benjamin's sudden flight from Berlin to Paris.

Der Dichter und die Langeweile

Der Dichter:

Tief geehrt und hoch berufen
was vermiss ich, der erschafft
Tönend von erhöhten Stufen
schwund in verbrachter Kraft.
Bilder kamen Bilder flichen
Doch mit einmal endlos nah
Fühl ich tief ein Gähnen ziehen
Wie denn, nie ein Leid geschah.

'Fritz Heinle was a poet, and the only one of them all whom I met not "in real life" but in his work. He died at nineteen and could be known in no other way . . . '[25] In his 'life' Benjamin had met Heinle in Freiburg in 1913 and their friendship, which was immediately intense ('we became friends in one night'), grew stronger in Berlin during their shared militancy in the Youth Movement. At the outbreak of the war, Heinle committed suicide with his girlfriend Rika Seligson and for his entire life Benjamin tried to find and publish the manuscripts of his poems. You can imagine the emotion with which I took the little notebook in my hands to photocopy before giving it back to Blumenthal. To be sure, the poems were nearly incomprehensible and could not be otherwise, since the language in which they were written was not properly a language but, as Benjamin says of youth, only a 'lament for lost greatness'. And every lament in truth tends towards the absence of language, borders upon muteness. But this is exactly what Benjamin found to be their special greatness.

In Heinle there was something like a tenacious will to be forgotten. Not only was Benjamin unable to recover the lost manuscripts, but when I met Scholem in Ascona in the summer of 1979 and immediately told him of the discovery of the poems, which in his *Story of a Friendship* he seems to believe had been lost, he told me that he knew Blumenthal had saved them. Since we cannot think that he intentionally wanted to hide them, this forgetting is not easy to explain. And when right after Blumenthal's death his widow called me over because, before leaving for England, she wanted to get rid of the papers of Benjamin's that her husband had saved, from these papers, which I still possess, the little blue-covered notebook in which Carla Seligson had copied the poems and from which I had transcribed them was missing. Despite my best efforts, it was impossible to find it.

In his essay on Dostoevsky's *The Idiot*, Benjamin evokes the figure of his friend when he writes that the life of Prince Myshkin remains unforgettable with no need of monuments or memorials and that it remains unforgettable even if no one bears witness for it.

What is unforgettable here is not what is eternally deposited in the archives of memory. On the contrary, what is truly unforgettable is not only that which demands not to be forgotten even if no one remembers it, but above all that which demands to be remembered *as forgotten*. More profound than any memory is the relation that the soul always maintains with what it has already forgotten because it could never be written down in the roll books of reminiscence. What is unforgettable is life itself, in all the body's infinite operations in every instant, which can't be known or remembered—what is unforgettable is the life 'with neither container nor form' that a 19-year-old poet took from himself in Berlin on 8 August 1914.

From then I began to follow the traces of Benjamin however and wherever I could, first in Paris in February 1980 where I met Jean Selz—who gave me his correspondence with Benjamin from August 1932 to April 1934 to publish—and Gisèle Freund. Selz was generous with information, though not without some hesitancies (he flatly refused to give me the address of his wife, whom I would have liked to interview—and since then I have suspected that she might have been the very woman with whom Benjamin became infatuated on Ibiza). Gisèle Freund had so many extraordinary things to say about herself and about photography that I quickly gave up on getting her to talk about Benjamin. I only regret not having followed her advice and gone to meet Helen Hessel, whose diaries I would read many

years later with constant wonder (I still have her address written in a notebook: Mme Hessel, 19 avenue du Géneral Leclerc, tel. 3311719).

Not long after that, I looked for and, thanks to some patient questioning, identified the house on Capri where Benjamin had lived in 1924. It was a small outbuilding to the villa of Baroness von Uexküll, the wife of the brilliant zoologist whose theories about the world of the tick would later give me so much to think about. With the same doggedness I photographed the houses where Benjamin had lived in Paris, until I began to realize that there was something unhealthy in that pursuit of the traces of a life that was, in any case, lost—like every life—forever.

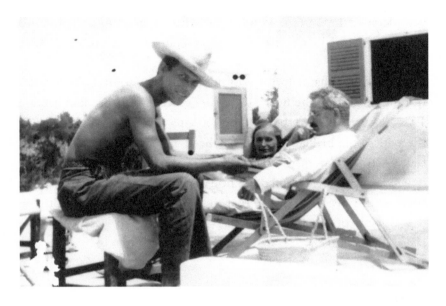

However, less than two years later a second and even more surprising encounter occurred in the Bibliotèque nationale in Paris, a place that Benjamin had frequented so intensely that he placed his planned *Arcades Project* under its sign. I have recounted elsewhere how, while searching for traces of Benjamin in Bataille's correspondence, I came across a letter that mentioned some manuscripts by Benjamin. A marginal note by Jean Bruno, who was then a curator at the BN, specified that those manuscripts were in the library. It took me a great deal of time to convince the curator of the manuscript department, who at first categorically dismissed the idea, that those manuscripts had to be in the BN. In fact, they were buried along with other uncatalogued treasures in the immense closet where, I learned a month later, the library kept manuscripts that it did not own, because they had been left there temporarily for safe keeping (in this case, by Bataille's widow).

It was with fear and trembling, but also with uncontainable joy, that one morning in June 1981 I watched the curator place on my table five yellow envelopes full of manuscripts going from the *Berlin Childhood* of the 1930s up to the book on Baudelaire that Benjamin was working on in the last two years of his life. Once again, in the minute and elegant handwriting—clear and legible when he wrote in French, but difficult to decipher when he was writing in German—Benjamin was materially, palpably present, almost as if he had led me by the hand to those rooms where, 40 years earlier, he had dwelled for so long.

In his last years in Paris, Benjamin had lived in such straightened circumstances that he could not afford to buy paper. Many of his notes are written down on the back of letters that he would cut up to use, like this one, on half of a letter from Jean Wahl, which records an appointment at the Closerie des Lilas together with Lionello Venturi.

What do I owe Benjamin? My debt to him is so incalculable that I cannot even attempt to answer. But there is one thing certainly: the ability to extract and tear what interests me from its historic context in order to restore life to it and let it act in the present. The operation must be done with all possible philological care but done fully and decisively. Without this, my incursions into theology, law, politics, and literature would not have been possible.

In this sense, Benjamin is the only writer whose work I have wanted, as far as my abilities allowed, to continue. Not that I saw his writings as some personal bequest that I was obligated to accept. Not only, as Hannah Arendt noted, has our inheritance been left to us by no testament, but it no longer makes sense for us to speak of any inheritance either to be received or to pass down. What makes his books so special is that Benjamin unhesitatingly broke with all inheritance and with the very idea of culture. His erudition is so deep that he can always discover the freshness of barbarities. This is why, in the history of culture, he prefers rags and dross, which, like a barbarian, he can use as he likes—and any waiting for the future is replaced not so much by a hope in the past as by the gesture that breaks the supposed continuity of history. Like Illich, he would never

Zum Begriff der Urgeschichte des neunzehnten Jahrhunderts

"Sommes-nous des êtres..." Andeutung der deterministischen Blanquis

Urgeschichte des neunzehnten Jahrhunderts als dialektisches Bild

Antithese zum ökonomen zu S'b begriffenen Dialektischen Bild

Urgeschichte des neunzehnten Jahrhunderts im Surrealistischen Zeit (das Leben der Verstorbenen)

Verhalten der Natur und Inanspruche zur Urgeschichte des neuen und inanspruche des Barocken Anschauungsformen des neunzehnten Jahrhunderts

à 9 h. — 9 h. ½ à la Closerie des Lilas. — Il croisque Lionello Venturi viendra aussi. — Si vous ne pouvez venir tôt, vous pouvez toujours encore venir à 11 heures. — et vous serions bien contents de vous voir. — moi je veux pour vous me dévêtir

Jean Wahl.

Si nous n'étions pas dans la 1ère salle, vous serions dans la seconde. —

Kapitel

I de arte poetica   der freie Schriftsteller
II Lutetia Parisiorum   die Masse
III taedium vitae   die Novität

I Spleen et idéal   Idee und Bild
II Tableaux parisiens   der Einsame und die Masse
III La mort   das Neue und Immergleiche
I Zeit und Ewigkeit
II Antike und Moderne
III ~~neue~~ Das Neue und Immergleiche.

have allowed the shadow of the future to fall on the concepts with which he sought to think the present and what has been; and like him, we also write for a humanity that no longer expects anything and from which we do not expect anything—for this reason we cannot ever miss our appointment with it.

When I look up at the firmament on summer nights, Benjamin is now a star with whom I speak in a lowered voice—no longer a guide or a model, but something like a *genius* or an angel to whom I have entrusted my life. Sometimes, if I call him, he remembers, distractedly, to look after it.

You cannot understand Benjamin's position in German culture of the early twentieth century if you do not place it in relation to the George circle, which, like an emblem, encapsulated the destiny of the best of those who saw themselves in the name of Germany. One aspect of the darker side of this emblem is the fact that the leading figures of the circle were Jews: Gundolf, Wolfskehl, Kantorowicz and the economist Edgar Salin. It has always astounded me that these Jewish men could have sought regeneration through Germany— even if it was George's 'secret Germany', which was essentially the German language and German poetry. Just as baffling to me is that in these same years—which were the very ones in which Hitler was developing his ideas about Judaism—Rosenzweig and Buber conceived their translation of the Torah in German, which to a Zionist like Scholem could rightly not have seemed any less anachronistic.

Between Zionism and the George circle, Benjamin's position seems incomparably more lucid. Despite recognizing the prophetic quality of George's poetry and the fact that masterpieces could be born out of his school, he clearly sees that the generation to whom his poems had offered refuge was predestined to death. 'This land,' he writes in a review with the significant title 'Against a Masterpiece', '[. . .] cannot be purified in the name of Germany—let alone the "secret Germany" that ultimately is nothing but the arsenal of official Germany, in which the magic hood of invisibility hangs next to the helmet of steel.'[26] The fact that George, taking up the liturgic-political apparatus staged by Wolters in *Herrschaft und Dienst* and later in the monumental hagiography of the poet published in 1929, referred to

the circle as a 'State' (*Staat*) betrays the secret bond that united the two Germanies. And I have always thought it a sign of this underground solidarity that the assassination attempt on Hitler on 20 July 1944 by an officer who came from the George circle (Claus von Stauffenberg, who in the photograph I have on a shelf in my library in Venice was barely 18 years old) was destined to fail.

The 'masterpiece' against which Benjamin wrote his review was *Der Dichter als Führer in der deutschen Klassik* (The poet as leader in German classicism) by Max Kommerell, perhaps the only critic of the twentieth century who is at all comparable to him. It is no accident that Kommerell produced his best work—his astonishing essay on Kleist ('Die Sprache und das Unaussprechliche') and his book on

Jean Paul—after having left the George circle. What immediately fascinated me about him was that his thought, like Benjamin's, tends to end up as a theory of gesture—of gesture as a non-signifying but expressive element, one which manifests itself in both language (the verse line as a 'linguistic gesture') and the face. That this has to do with something not directed towards communication is proven by the fact that 'even a face that has no witnesses has its mimicry' and that the gestures that leave the deepest marks on a face are precisely those that tell the story of its solitary moments. And if speech itself, for Kommerell, is a gesture—indeed, the original gesture—this therefore means that what is essential to language is a non-communicative moment, a muteness embedded within man's being a speaker—that is to say, his dwelling in language is not turned solely towards the exchange of messages but is above all gestural and expressive.

This is the starting point of the theory of gesture that, by connecting it with Benjamin's idea of pure means, I sought to develop in 'Notes on Gesture' and on which I continue to reflect. The preliminary condition for understanding gesture is a clear distinction between the signifying moment and the expressive moment. Expression is a suspension of the signifying relation ('this means that') which, in the very act in which it deactivates that relation, shows it as such. What the gesture exhibits and brings to expression is not something unsayable but speech itself, the very being-in-language of man. This is why it has nothing at all to say. The definition of philosophy that I have drawn from this still seems convincing to me: if being-in-language is not something that can be communicated with sentences and propositions, the gesture will then always be the gesture of not figuring language out; it will always be a 'gag', in the proper sense of the term, which first means something stuck in the mouth to impede speech and then the improvisation of an actor to fill in for a memory lapse, an inability to speak. 'Every great philosophical text is the gag that exhibits language itself, man's very being-in-language as a gigantic lapse of memory, as an incurable speech impediment.'

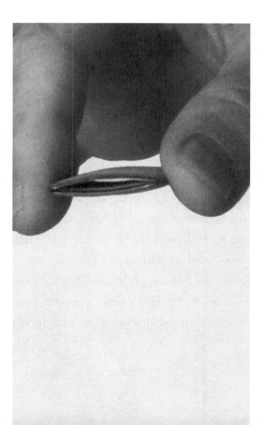

Gesture is therefore also like the gallinaceous voice of Pulcinella, which is not a voice but, as English puppeteers call it, an 'unknown language', an artifice that, as Bruno Leone showed me, the guarattellaro produces using the pivetta, a sort of coil made with two pieces of brass held together with a thread that is slipped under his palate and can sometimes end up being swallowed. Pulcinella's voice—his gesture—shows that there is still something to say when it is no longer possible to speak, just as his lazzi show that there is still something to do when all action has become impossible.

Among those in the George circle, the one I have always unconditionally admired is Norbert von Hellingrath, who died at Verdun at 28 years old. To him we owe—after his discovery of the manuscripts of the last hymns and translations of Pindar in the Stuttgart library in 1909—the edition of the poems Hölderlin was unable to complete but which had a decisive influence on a generation, and not only in Germany. If I feel particularly close to him, though, it is rather because of the extraordinary understanding of poetry that he expressed in his lectures on Hölderlin. Taking up the Alexandrine distinction between *harmonia austera* ('harsh technique') and *harmonia glaphura* ('smooth technique'), he identifies in the former (which he calls *harte Fügung*, 'hard articulation') the characteristic feature of Hölderlin's late poetry. What defines the hard articulation is not so much parataxis as it is the tendency to isolate single words from their semantic context in the discourse by multiplying caesurae and enjambments, thus restoring them to their status as names. 'Hard articulation,' he writes, 'does everything possible to exalt the word itself, impressing it in the listener's hearing and pulling it as far as possible from the associative context of images and feelings to which it belongs.'[27] This means that Hölderlin's late hymns have an anti-semantic tension running through them, one that undoes meaning in order to reach the pure word, the name severed from any semantic connection. In the notes to his translation of Oedipus, Hölderlin thus speaks of a caesura or 'antirhythmic interruption' that, by slowing down the succession of words and images, makes appear 'no longer the alternation of the representations, but representation itself.' In

contrast to what happens with 'smooth articulation' (*glatte Fügung*), in which the words flow together and match with one another in the context of the discourse, here the verse line is reduced to a succession of odd bits and pieces, to a field of ruins from which single terms emerge, sometimes even just conjunctions (such as—in ferocious isolation—the adversative conjunction *aber*, 'but').

The opposition between the two types of articulation is not valid merely for Hölderlin: it configures the language of poetry as a field of tensions traversed by two inverse currents, one that moves towards the name, the other that binds and holds the terms in a discursive nexus. And so it may be possible to distinguish poets according to which of these two types of *harmonia* predominates in their work: at one extreme there will be the hymn—which is always the celebration of a name—and at the other end the elegy, which laments the impossibility of the hymn and the fleetingness of names. And it is possible that truly great poets can be counted among the adepts of the harsh technique, from Pindar (the champion of the *harmonia austera* among the ancients) to Arnault Daniel (the sestina being nothing but a spiral vortex of six names) up to Mallarmé, who pushes the isolation of words all the way to their illegible dissemination in the pages of the *Coup de dés*.

Analogous considerations can be made for the language of philosophy, whose field is divided between philosophers of the name— the progenitor of whom is Plato: the idea is nothing but the 'name itself'—and philosophers of discourse, gathered under the aegis of Aristotle, who tenaciously privileges the apophantic *logos*, which can be true or false (the name, by definition, escapes this dichotomy). The former seek to direct the currents of discourse towards the river mouth of the name (in this sense, the dense dialectical exchange of the Socratic dialogue is a complicated device aimed at bringing forth the potentiality of the *onoma*, that is, the idea: the Beautiful, the Just, the Good . . .), while the latter, on the contrary, seek to dissolve and liquidate the name in the rhythm of the discourse.

As different as the writing strategies with which I have had to contend may be, I nevertheless do not hesitate to place myself among the adepts of *the harmonia austera*: we have not been given language solely that we might say something about something; language is above all a tension towards the name, the liberation of the *onoma* from the endless discursive plots of *logos*.

On one shelf of my bookcase in Venice, I keep, next to his books, a photograph of Giorgio Pasquali, a photo that has caught him in a gesture of that mental happiness that his students have described. For me, this writer—who was as extravagant as his pages and is certainly among the greatest Italian writers of the twentieth century—is the emblem of one of my most enduring temptations—philology, which I have never been able to separate from philosophy. In a letter from 1921, Benjamin compares it to an ascetic discipline that promises the joys that the Neoplatonic philosophers sought in contemplation.[28]

What the philologist mystically contemplates is, obviously, language, but more specifically, according to Benjamin, it is terminology, exactly that aspect of language—the name—that the poet's *harmonia austera* isolates and exalts. This is why, in its extreme form, it resembles a magical practice that 'casts its spell on the investigator' and makes him forget the historical context in which his object—the text—must be situated and constructed for it to be intelligible.[29]

For Pasquali, it is just this dialectic between the text in its unattainable, almost magical original fixity and the history that has transmitted it that constitutes the meaning of philology. In this sense, the title of his masterpiece, *Storia della tradizione e critica del testo* (History of the tradition and textual criticism), speaks eloquently: only a critical knowledge of the tradition that has carried it down to us allows us to enter the text that we want to read; but this is not—or nearly never is—the original; it is, rather, what we reach by climbing back against the grain of the living history of its tradition. In Lachmann's stemmatics, the archetype to which the philologist traces back the countless and differing manuscripts is not the original, but is itself already disfigured and corrupted, and it is indeed only by comparing the corruptions common to many manuscripts that their archetype could be identified.

This, for me, is the incomparable political lesson of philology. Its teaching is that without exception we receive our culture—like our language—through a historical tradition, but this tradition has always already been knowingly or unknowingly altered and corrupted. Even when (as with texts less distant in time) we have access to documents written in the writer's own hand, these—as anyone who has had such documents before him knows—already contain multiple authorial variants, and in order to choose among them we must once again venture out into a philological exercise. The original in its truth does not lie in the past, but has its place in the present, in the instant in which the philologist—or the philologist that every politically aware reader must be—battles hand-to-hand with the tradition, in what Heidegger rightly defined as an inexorable and all-out 'destruction'.

For me, the philological principles stated by Pasquali—like that of the *lectio difficilior*—have a genuinely political significance for exactly this reason. 'Difficilior et obscurior lectio anteponenda est ei, in qua omnia tam plana sunt et extricata, ut librarius quisque facile intelligere ea potuerit', which can be translated with a few adjustments as: 'The more difficult and obscure reading must be preferred to the one in which everything has been made so simple and clear that any fool can understand it straight away.'

Reading Pasquali's book on the Platonic letters—to which he returned to work shortly before his death—convinced me of the authenticity of the *Seventh Letter*, this incomparable text in which this man who had written unsurpassed masterpieces of Attic prose declares outright that 'of the problems with which I am concerned . . . there is no writing of mine about these matters, nor will there ever be one' and that a serious writer cannot truly take anything he writes seriously.[30] And yet, in a late work he compares his dialogues to tragedies and claims for himself the standing of a poet. ('We're tragedians ourselves, and our tragedy is the finest and best we can create . . . So we are poets like yourselves, composing in the same *genre*, and your competitors as artists.')[31] This poetic intention was so obvious to the ancients that, as early as the first editions, they collected the Platonic dialogues in tetralogies.

A philosopher who does not take on a poetic problem is not a philosopher. This does not, however, mean that philosophical writing has to be poetic. Rather, it must contain the dispersed traces of a poetic writing, must in some way exhibit its farewell to poetry. Plato did this by composing a large and wonderful literary work, only then to declare it devoid of seriousness and worth, and by always intentionally contaminating tragedy with mime and comedy. For us, who can no longer write dialogues, the task is even more arduous. If writing always betrays thought and if philosophy cannot, however, simply renounce the word, then in writing the philosopher will have to seek the point at which writing disappears in the voice, must chase it, in every discourse, to the voice that was never written—to the idea. The idea is the point at which signifying language is abolished in the name. And writing is philosophical if it accepts that it will always find itself without a language in front of the voice and without a voice in front of the language.

I have almost always lived in houses that did not belong to me and, as it happens, I have often had to abandon them. I wonder how I have been able, and am still able, to write in different studios and live in many places. It is certainly an exorbitant tribute I pay to the spirit of such rootless times—but I believe that they all in truth make up a single studio, spread out in space and time. This is why—although I have at times woken up and not known exactly where I was—I can recognize the same elements and the same objects in them, though slightly moved around or changed. Thus, pieces of furniture and images from the studio on Vicolo del Giglio survive in the studio on Via Corsini. The dresser under which I keep the archive of my published writings has remained identical in the two places, and at times, while looking for a book, I seem to reencounter the gestures of those lost days, testament to the fact that the studio, as an image of potentiality, is something utopian that gathers within itself different times and places.

The little Pulcinella propped up on the dresser on Via Corsini belonged to Totò and was given to me by Goffredo Fofi. My relationship with the characters of the Commedia dell'Arte, and in particular with Pulcinella, goes so far back in time that I would not be able place it in a chronology. As far as we know from the written testimonies and images of them that have survived—from Watteau to Tiepolo, from Callot to Magnasco—Harlequin, Scaramouche, Pulcinella, Colombina and the other characters of the Commedia

dell'Arte touch upon a unique ethical dimension that is freer and deeper than the one tragedy has passed down to modern morals. Neither flesh and blood individuals nor simple types, these characters eternally oscillate between reality and virtuality, life and dream, singularity and generality. And if in tragedy, as Aristotle says, men do not act to imitate character but assume their action through character and thus become responsible for it, comic personages on the contrary act only in imitation of their character in such a way that their actions are ultimately indifferent to them and do not remotely touch them. This is why their actions are changed into lazzi, the meaning of which is only the liberation of the character from any possible imputation of responsibility. Though the plot would like to entangle him, Pulcinella never lives through the deeds and episodes of his life—rather, he lives through only his blessed impossibility of living, just as his gestures remain perpetually beyond or before action and his words perennially beyond or before any communication of a meaning. This is why, in Benjamin's words, the comic character holds up the clear vision of man's natural innocence in opposition to the dark dogma of the guilt of creatures.

(A marionette of Pulcinella, hand carved by a young Neapolitan artisan in Venice, now rests on the small Japanese stand in my Venice studio, between the photograph of Bergamín and a photograph of my mother.)

On the fireplace on Vicolo del Giglio, next to Titan's *Nymph and Shepherd*, which I had seen in the Kunsthistorisches Museum of Vienna in the summer of 1980 and happened to write about many years later, you can glimpse a postcard with the image of a beautiful canvas by Giovanni Serodine kept in the Biblioteca Ambrosiana in Milan. The title listed in catalogues is *Allegory of Science*, which was probably suggested by the instruments strewn across the table in the foreground.

However, what seems decisive to me is the gesture of the female figure who unmistakably aims the stream of milk jetting from her right breast towards her own mouth. That is to say, this is an allegory of self-nourishing, of the soul's self-nourishing that Plato discusses in the *Seventh Letter* when he reminds Dion's friends that the things about which he is seriously concerned cannot simply be said like the others; rather, only after we have spoken of them and lived with them for a long time, they suddenly light up in the soul like a spark shooting from a fire, which 'nourishes itself [*auto heauto ēdē trephei*]'.[32]

This image has a long and sometimes cloying lineage. But what does it mean to nourish oneself? What is a light that feeds itself? A flame that no longer needs fuel? I believe the image refers to the soul's relation to its ardour, to that which sets it alight. That the flame nourishes itself means that when a certain limit is surpassed the soul becomes the fire that sets it alight, becomes one with it. It is not by chance that Serodine chose for this such a simple and material figure—the milk of the maternal breast. In the process of nourishing—in any kind of nourishing, spiritual or bodily—there is a threshold at which the process reverses direction and turns back towards itself. Food can nourish only if at a certain point it is no longer something other than us, only if we have—as they say—*assimilated* it; but this means—to exactly the same degree—that we are assimilated to it. The same thing happens with the light of knowledge: it always arises from outside, but there arrives a moment when inside and outside meet and we can no longer tell them apart. At this point, the fire ceases to consume us, 'it now consumes itself': *ignis ardens non comburens*, as Titian wrote at the bottom of the *Annunciation* of San Salvador—this time an allegory of the act of creation.

I was still living in the studio on Vicolo del Giglio when, on 22 February 1988, I started teaching at the University of Macerata with a course on Heidegger. The years at Macerata were especially lively because of how much I learned from teaching (and thus, in the last analysis, from the students), which is the only reason teaching is worth it. And it is there that a small group of students and I founded a publishing house, where I sometimes still publish. And it was at Macerata where I met Stefano Scodanibbio at a concert during the occupation. To be sure, by reinventing the use of harmonics, Stefano gave the double bass back its own voice, which had until then been submerged, as he said, under the babbling of foreign voices. But only someone who saw Stefano play can attest to how, amid the most unprecedented novelty, an archaic dimension would suddenly emerge, as if the double bass were for him the 'path in the sky' along which the Siberian shaman leads the sacrificial animal. As if his whole body and the whole bass melted together into an antediluvian being, at once rigorous and ferocious, in which music and dance are restored to their original unity. We worked together on his piece *Heaven on Earth* for two dancers, fifteen children and ten musicians, for which I was able to engage Alexandra Gilbert, an extraordinary dancer whom I had seen dance nude in Berlin in *Foi* by Sidi Larbi Cherkaoui.

My friendship with Stefano and Maresa accompanied me up until his untimely death—evenings in the house in Pollenza, where he would cook the pasillas which he particularly loved and which would give to the pasta an unforgettable fragrance of wood and raisins, or travelling around the world—Stefano could never get enough of travelling (or of anything else for that matter), above all in his Mexico, which he brought me to discover in 1995 and where he wanted, in the end, to die.

I don't know why remembering Stefano brings to mind my brief meeting, at 18 years old, with Igor Stravinsky in the house of the director of the Filarmonica Romana, whose son studied piano and was a friend of mine. His mother took advantage of Stravinsky's presence in Rome to ask him to listen to her son at the piano and he had asked me to be there for encouragement. I have never forgotten the sight of that small man of nearly 80 years—but with a face bristling with life—who stood silently listening to my friend's playing. It was as if the hesitant gaze that I fixed upon that famous musician, visibly bored by the task asked of him but so engulfed in his genius, measured the infinite distance that still separated me from myself, uncertain and waiting.

From my years at Macerata I have kept the notebooks in which Sandro M., without knowing Greek or German, copied out passages of Plato and Aristotle, Rilke or Heidegger. The gesture of a boy who feverishly, devotedly copied out a language he could not read or write inspires a sort of reverential fear in me. I have always thought that this stubborn, patient copying hid something like an enigma, as if by sticking purely to the letter, Sandro—or a *daimon* in him— understood something of those texts that escaped me and that was impossible to formulate other than in the obstinate gesture of following. As if, in this way, he reached that illegible element that had been transcribed in those hieroglyphics, the illegible from which and towards which every word written by human beings travels.

UND SO DRÄNGEN WIR UNS UND WOLLEN ES LEISTEN,

WOLLENS ~~MR~~ ENTHALTEN IN UNSERN EINFACHEN HÄNDEN,

IM ÜBERFÜLLTEREN BLICK UND IM SPRACHLOSEN HERZEN.

WOLLEN ES WERDEN. — WEM ES GEBEN? AM LIEBSTEN

ALLES BEHALTEN FÜR IMMER ... ACH, IN DEN ANDERN BEZUG,

WEHE, WAS NIMMT MAN HINÜBER? NICHT DAS ANSCHAUN,

DAS HIER

LANGSAM ERLERNTE, UND KEIN HIER EREIGNETES. KEINS,

ALSO DIE SCHMERZEN. ALSO VOR ALLEM DAS SCHWERSEIN,

ALSO DER LIEBE LANGE ERFAHRUNG, — ALSO

LAUTER UNSÄGLICHES. ABER SPÄTER,

UNTER DEN STERNEN, WAS SOLLS: DIE SIND BESSER UNSÄGLICH.

BRINGT DOCH DER WANDERER AUCH VOM HANGE DES

BERGRANDS

NICHT EINE HAND VOLL ERDE INS TAL, DIE ALLEN UNSÄGLICHE,

SONDERN

EIN ERWORBENES WORT, REINES, DEN GELBEN UND BLAUN

ENZIAN. SIND WIR VIELLEICHT HIER, UM ZU SAGEN: HAUS,

BRÜCKE, BRUNNEN, TOR KRUG, OBSTBAUM, FENSTER, —

HÖCHSTENS: SÄULE, TURM ... ABER ZU SAGEN, VERSTEHS,

And as if, once again, the truth could be expressed only on the condition that it cannot be heard, written as long as it cannot be read.

In my studio in Venice, in the corner of a shelf in the library, a photograph recalls the afternoon in October 1992 when, in the backroom of a cafe in the Alameda district of Seville, I witnessed something that I will never forget: a fiesta flamenco improvised by two extraordinary cantaores, Manuel Rodríguez, known as Pies de Plomo, and Enrique Montes. The former a perfect exemplar of oral culture ('my *trascendencia*,' he told me, 'is Italian'), the latter more reserved and elegant. Two very different singing styles—and yet, both of an

absolute purity. Little by little, the congenial atmosphere, the jaleo and the manzanilla make them slip into the song, as if it were not up to them when to begin; but once they get started, the cantaores cannot stop themselves in the ever-tighter entwining of their call and response. Such was their enthusiasm that, while the guitarist was taking a break, Pies de Plomo sang without music, banging his knuckles on the table.

No one there—they told me at the end—had ever seen such an exalting fiesta, such a total *continuum* of song. But what made it incomparable for me was that it gave the lie to the wretched convention that says that what should be a simple, joyous, common experience must be separated out into a spectacle, that everything that is worth living for and that, as such, has to be shared must be transformed into culture and shown on a stage in front of a paying audience.

This is why I look upon concerts and festivals with horror; this is why I have less and less desire to talk at conferences; this is why I will never forget that cafe in Alameda, just as I will never forget the evenings in Pollenza when Stefano, after cooking pasillas for us, picked up the double bass and began to play.

Propped on the lower-left shelf there is a photograph of Giorgio Colli, whose work, along with that of Enzo Melandri and Gianni Carchia, will certainly remain as a testament of Italian thought in the twentieth century. Of others, who get presented on television as the greatest philosophers of our time, absolutely nothing will remain.

In the house on Via Corsini, two cabinets hold the collection of old illustrated children's books that I collected for some years beginning in the mid-seventies and continued up to the point when I realized I had to stop because, as with all collections, it was becoming obsessive. It had certainly begun because of my particular fondness for everything that has to do with childhood, which in exactly those years I had theoretically formulated in *Infancy and History*.

For some time I had known the Dutch anatomist Lodewijk Bolk's extraordinary pamphlet 'On the Problem of Anthropogenesis' (1926), which contains an absolutely innovative intuition about the question of the 'becoming human' of the primate of the genus *homo*. In his research on comparative anatomy, Bolk realized that the human resembled not so much an adult primate but primate fetus—that is to say, that the somatic characteristics of the human are fetal characteristics that have become permanent. 'What is a transitional stage in the ontogenesis of other Primates has become a terminal stage in Man.' Bolk calls this process 'fetalization' and from it he draws the conclusion that from an evolutionary point of view the human is a 'Primate-fetus that has become sexually mature' and that the human species is the arrest of the infantile stage of an ape.[33]

To the fetalization theory Bolk adds another hypothesis that is decisive for understanding the nature and destiny (or absence of destiny) of man: that of the retardation or inhibition of development. The principle of retardation, Bolk writes, dominates not only the course of the human's development as a species (phylogeny) but also the entire course of a human being's individual life (ontogeny). There is no mammal that grows as slowly as the human, nor one that becomes an adult so long after being born. Since our development is so retarded, human parents must take care of their little fetuses for years (while other animals abandon them relatively soon), they must band together to build houses and shelters and progressively give form to that exosomatic civilization that distinguishes the human species from other animal species. The hypothesis of fetalization and retardation allows us, that is, not only to understand the somatic characteristics of the human but also to explain our peculiar history in the animal kingdom and the typically human development of a cultural tradition through language. Exosomatic civilization came about to make up for our somatic immaturity. Only a being condemned to a state of prolonged immaturity could have invented language. (Furthermore, this allows us to understand the curious fact that language learning has remained tenaciously tied to the infantile condition.)

Perhaps it was some testimony of this special meaning of the infantile condition that I sought in these old illustrated children's books. Precisely because they tend to repress their embarrassing fetal nature, adults look at children with caution and diffidence and confine them to a special sphere—the nursery or the school—where they must be attentively watched and rigorously educated in order to contain their threatening totipotency. At a certain point in their history, humans, forgetting the grace that every vagueness contains, began to

ALFABETO REGOLARE

A B C D E F G H
I J K L M N O P
Q R S T U V W
X Y Z

— Tutti i più grandi scienziati hanno cominciato così.
— Allora, disse la signorina Mimì, incominciamo.

Φ φ

φωλιά

Ὁ Γιωργάκης μὲ
Πιπίτσα βρῆκαν
μιὰ φωλιά.

Χ χ

χῆνες

Ἡ Λιλίκα φοβᾶται
τῆς χῆνες. Κλαίει
καὶ φωνάζει.

transform their fetal indeterminateness into a destiny and into a force capable of dominating and destroying the world. In the figures of those books, the infantile world thus appears as a dumfounded and stunned universe that is at once subjected to the ceaseless vigilance of adults and assiduously and guiltily trying to escaping it.

This is particularly evident in ABC books, of which I have quite a few in my collection, in a variety of languages. Here, where the child is about to leap over the fatal threshold to the world of writing, his or her understandable hesitation and terror coexist for a moment with the promises and splendour of the Word finally mastered. In any case, even in books that are not ABC books, the child is always astonished or in difficulty, or absorbed in his or her toys, or in the act of committing the cruellest misdeeds. That is to say, as in reality, he or she is a foreigner who in no way belongs to the same species as adults, even if today this heterogeneity—as has also happened with women—tends gradually to fade away.

The most precious book in my collection is the first edition of *Pinocchio* in the first year (1881) of the *Giornale per i bambini*, in which Pinocchio does not end up becoming a good boy but dies miserably, hanged by two murderers: 'Little by little his eyes grew dim; and although he felt death approaching, he nonetheless still continued to hope that at any moment some compassionate soul would pass by and help him. But when, after waiting and waiting, he saw that nobody showed up, absolutely nobody, then he remembered his poor father again. "Oh dear father! . . . if only you were here!"

And he had no breath to say anything else. He closed his eyes, opened his mouth, stretched out his legs, and, after giving a great shudder, he remained there as though frozen stiff.'[34]

But the book that I love best is perhaps the first edition of Tommaso Landolfi's *Il principe infelice*, with its astonishing images by Sabino Profeti, a painter who might never have existed, since the only work of his we know are these illustrations. I still have the copy I was given as a child, the images of which must have had such a strong effect on my imagination that I had to include them in the second edition of *Idea of Prose*.

Landolfi never ceased to torment himself over two mysteries: chance and language. In his *Dialogo dei massimi sistemi*—a high point in Italian literature of those years—the two intersect in a poem that chance has led the author to write in a non-existent language or— and this is the same thing—a language that he believes only he knows: 'Aga magéra difúra natun gua mesciún . . . ' But as the first of his *Racconti impossibili* shows, the vocabulary of every language in reality contains within it a non-existent language, which no one— or nearly no one—knows—and this is precisely the language of poetry (similar to the dead language of which Pascoli was enamoured). In the same years, a friend of Landolfi's in the cafes of Florence, Antonio Delfini, followed the same dream, finishing *Il ricordo della Basca* with an entirely unintelligible poem (which in truth, as I happened to discover, is written in Basque: 'Ene izar maitea / ene

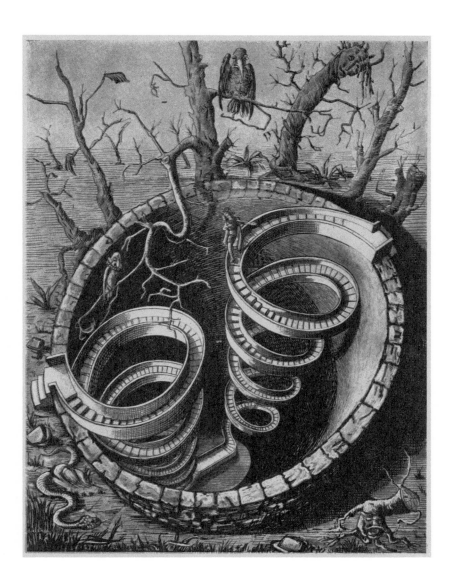

charmaggaria . . . '). Seeking by chance and against chance a language that doesn't exist—this is the game of chance to which Landolfi dedicated his life.

On the page of one of the ABC books—perhaps like the one that Pinocchio sells in order to go and see the puppet theatre—there is a list of the simple syllables (*ba be bi bo bu, ca ce ci co cu, da de di do du*, etc.) that provided Italo Calvino (and Georges Perec before him) with the material with which he could always draw, after the example of Roussel, a short tale or anecdote. I recall his evident enjoyment while retelling the one he drew from *la le li lo lu*: 'Putting his finger to his head, Nietzsche explained to Lou von Salomé that his essential quality was intellectual order: "I've a wing there, Lou [*L'ale lí l'ho, Lu*]!" ' The endeavour is symmetrically opposite—but it is, at base, the same: to wrack your brains to give a meaning to what has none—instead of removing it from what has too much.

I have often dreamed of finding the Book, the absolute and perfect Book—the one that we have consciously or less consciously sought everywhere, in every bookstore, in every library. It is an illustrated book, like the old children's books in my collection, and in my dream I hold it in my hands and leaf through it with growing joy. We ceaselessly continue to search like this for years, until we realize that that book doesn't exist anywhere and that the only way to find it is to write it ourselves.

I have been accompanied in every one of my studios by a photograph of Robert Walser—and in the book of mine that is particularly dear to me, he is entrusted with the cipher or *shibboleth* of the coming (and, at the same time, forever departing) community. Walser's style—indeed, his mannerism—is inimitable because it hangs suspended over an abyss into which no one today could fall, for in the meantime it has become the little apartment—nihilism—in which we all live. At the edge of this chasm, Walser's characters instead are able, with a sort of transcendental balance, to walk around and almost dance. Their manners are manners and gestures of nothingness, pantomimes and circus dances that, like all pantomimes, contain an initiatory element, are a mystery in the purely theatrical sense of the term. But in this initiation, there is no space for any revelation; there is nothing at all to learn. This is why, as in Kafka, the complicity with nothingness has something comical about it. Just as the metaphysical youngster in 'I Have Nothing' only repeats the phrase 'I'd be glad to give you something if I had anything,'[35] so Walser's prose says over and over again: 'I'd be glad to teach you something if I had anything to teach'—and this lack of any pedagogical vocation is his most arduous, most vital doctrine.

A commonplace idea about Walser would see him—like a student of the infamous Benjamenta Institute—as submissive and obedient to the point of servility and self-effacement or, as written on his clinical charts in Waldau, 'completely without needs', 'calm, imperturbable, detached, impassive'. He is irremediably lost, but he does

not remember it or suffer for it. Indeed, quite the opposite—he seems incurably cheerful. He writes without goal or profit, 'for the cat', as he says, which is 'a type of factory or industrial establishment for which writers, day after day and hour after hour, work faithfully and busily.' Stories like the wings of a butterfly, which serve no purpose but to fly, but not too high.

To be sure, Walser has nothing to improve and nothing to save. But his holiness, if we can speak of holiness, comes from a vision that is so steadfastly unsullied by the evil surrounding him that it can be mistaken—as also happened with Kafka—for total complicity. The truth, though, is quite otherwise. He has clearly seen—as happened to Hölderlin before him—that the world in which he found himself had become purely and simply invisible to him. And this was something he could not have any illusions about improving. Prophets admonish and denounce, but those who have seen the form that horror has taken in our times no longer want to blame or condemn, and our prophecy is today of this type. 'To know so much and to have seen so much / that one has nothing, absolutely nothing to say.' This is why, without batting an eyelash, he willingly spent nearly 30 years in an asylum, just as he uncomplainingly accepted such diagnoses as 'hebephrenic' and 'catatonic', which that world assigned to him.

'I quite liked being in a sickroom,' he writes with perfect lucidity. 'One lies there like a felled tree, without having to lift a finger. Desires sleep like a child weary from playing. One feels as if in a cloister, or in the antechamber of death . . . I am convinced that Hölderlin was not nearly so unhappy in the last thirty years of his life as the literature professors make him out to be. Dreaming the days away in some modest corner, without constant demands, is certainly not martyrdom. People just make it one!'[36] In a short prose piece from 1926 (three years before being hospitalized in Waldau), he writes: 'Hölderlin saw fit, that is, found it tactful, to lose his common sense in his fortieth year.'[37]

The tower in the carpenter's house in Tübingen and the little hospital room in Herisau: these are two places on which we should never tire of meditating. What was accomplished within those walls—the refusal of reason on the part of two peerless poets—is the strongest objection that has ever been raised against our civilization. And once again, in the words of Simone Weil: only those who have accepted the most extreme state of social degradation can speak the truth.

I also believe that, in the world that befell me, everything that seems desirable to me and seems worth living for can find a place only in a museum or a prison or a mental hospital. I know this with absolute certainty, but unlike Walser I have not had the courage to follow out all its consequences. In this sense, my relation to the facts of my existence that could not happen is just as—if not more—important than my relation with those that did. In our society, everything that is allowed to happen is of little interest, and an authentic autobiography should rather occupy itself with facts that did not.

'I'm going with Herr Benjamenta into the desert. I just want to see if one can live and breathe and be in the wilderness too, willing good things and doing them, and sleeping and dreaming at night. What's all this. I don't want to think of anything more now. Not even of God? No! God will be with me. What should I need to think of him? God goes with thoughtless people'[38]

For a while I had a photograph of a girl urinating pinned up on a shelf in my Venice studio. I don't think I would like explain the reasons for this. I wouldn't be able to—it isn't possible now, because in our world paradise and hell are in the same place, separated for only a brief instant—and we cannot always perceive that instant. As Benjamin knew, the elements of the final state are dispersed in the present in shady and ridiculous forms. But this doesn't mean we have to forget them—even if I sometimes think it might not be necessary to imagine them.

There is, however, something I want to say about it, even if only in the form of a consideration of the historical type. Urination is one of the functions of life defined—with a disparaging term which goes back to the commentators of Aristotle (who hated plants)—as 'vegetative' (for me plants are rather a form of life in every way superior to ours: they live in a perpetual dream, feeding on light). The separation of vegetative life from sensitive and intellectual life is the operation that serves as the foundation for the anthropological machine of the West, with all the miseries and successes that the latter entails. Even if resuscitation techniques have made this separation practically possible and allowed for the indefinite maintenance of a body suspended in this caesura, for me vegetative life remains indistinguishable from relational life, and urination is entirely homogeneous with thought.

From September 1971 to June 1974, I lived in Paris in a studio at rue Jacob 16, just next door to the house where Wagner had lived. Two large French doors opened out onto the garden where Natalie Barney, by then in her nineties and still healthy, lived. She was the American writer who in the first decades of the twentieth century had scandalized Paris with her lesbian love affairs and the woman to whom Marina Tsvetaeva had addressed her 'Letter to the Amazon'. I recall when she died in February 1972 seeing an elderly woman in the abandoned garden burning a pile of letters and papers that must have belonged to her. But what has stayed with me most vividly from those years in Paris is certainly my friendship with Claudio Rugafiori and Italo Calvino.

Claudio is perhaps the only person who ever performed the function of a teacher for me, perhaps because he was the only one who did not seem to come from anywhere or to be going anywhere. The other places he invented (India, China) did not serve as somewhere for him to go but as places to erase every possible place. The material circumstances of his life—which indeed existed: he lived in rue Mazarine with an older woman—seemed entirely irrelevant to him, like his clothes, which were always the same, always dark (a uniform, he would say). His endless knowledge, on the other hand, was always connected to a vital exigency, like in the writers of the *Grand Jeu*—

especially Daumal—on whom he had worked intensely. Following these exigencies, he moved with ease in sinology as well as the Upanishads, from Artaud to Marcel Mauss, in Spinoza's geometric Latin as well as the Celtic fantasies of the *Voyage of St Brendan*. All academic aims were foreign to him: like a shaman he flew about the immense savanna of his knowledge following a compass that a young friend of mine, Emanuele Dattilo, would later compare to Granet's 'evocative singularities'. 'Knowledge,' Granet writes about China, 'consists in constituting collections of evocative singularities,' fragmentary and inconclusive images of totalities of which they take part but to which they nevertheless absolutely cannot be reduced, totalities which they nevertheless contract and condense within themselves as an emblem. And yet these images cannot exist except in a group; they cannot exist entirely in isolation from other singularities, with which they find themselves communicating. Perhaps Claudio himself (the 'legendary Rugafiori', as Italo Calvino said when I mentioned his name for the first time) was a similar collection of evocative singularities, which from time to time he would show according to an unpredictable urgency that never failed to surprise his interlocutor.

Nothing can provide a more fitting image of this most peculiar cognitive method than the pages Claudio would send us when, together with Italo, we began to work on a journal we were planning but which would never come to fruition (recently Emanuele, Elenio, Nicoletta and I tried to ascertain its currency and, at the same time, impossibility). Some of the journal's key subjects were those we were

A) FASCICOLO TESTO

captare (mdos)   4 parti   "la città del tutto"
                      2 metà
                      reciprocazione?
                      iterativo o gnomico

1ª Metà

INVENZIONE   ≠   CRITICA(immaginazione cr.)   "Parler c'est à la fois
                                                      agir et penser".(Mauss,
                                                      a partire da Aristotele)
lo specchio   i mostri   (invenzione = ripetizione
magico: pre=   di una visione?)
sente, assente?
utile,inutile?   Gioia, non 'io cristallo'
(riflessione)   (rifrazione)   (tipo cristallino).(Klee
                        o formalizzazione   oppure Spinoza)

                                                      "Comprendre. Voir."(Tzara)
VAGHEZZA   -------   ARCHITETTURA   etc.
ESTENSIONE   -------   SOPRAVVIVENZA

2ª Metà

Riquadro del "poco" (il meno possibile): l'edu=
    cazione.   EDUCAZIONE ="une sugges=
(Riquadro : rifiuto di ogni cosa non "mentaliz=   tion définitive"(Mauss)
    zabile", poi, una cosa alla volta = il meno
    possibile.) O da meditare o da spiegare.   leggi organizzatrici: in=
Paradigmi. L'esemplificazione. (Exemplum dici=   cominciare con esempi, non
    tur quod sequamur aut vitemus.) - trattare di   con ipotesi (Klee)
    una cosa, per poter illustrare tutte le cose.
                                                       etc.
XXXXXXXXXXXXXXXXX XXXX Rubriche possibili:
1. La scrematura : le formule.
    oppure:
    La definizione (o la descrizione)
2. La crestomazia (commentata o meno). Testi e
    immagini (es. jeux de ficelle, diagrammi, etc.)
    oppure:
    Il testo e l'oggetto: la spiegazione (prope=
    deutica)
3. XXXXXXX La critica (escl. di un testo 'pubbli=
    co; cioè scolastico, etc.)
    oppure:
    La lettura (di un'opera,come dialogo)

calling 'Italian categories', which, on one of those pages, are reflected in the oppositions 'vagueness / architecture', 'invention / critique', 'extension / survival' (or, in Italo's *Six Memos for the Next Millennium*, 'quickness / lightness'). Once again, these are not substantial definitions but have to do with the ability to institute and perceive analogies. I do not know if Claudio knew Enzo Melandri's book *La linea e il circolo*, which I would read with passion years later. Melandri, too, wanted to restore the prestige of a form of knowledge—analogy—that Western philosophy has constantly repressed. But for Claudio the analogic sensibility functioned like a sort of physiognomic instinct that unfailingly allowed him to redesign, by way of resemblances, the cartography of a given field of knowledge. An example of this are the lists of texts that he suggested for the journal, which unexpectedly drew together Plautus' *Mostellaria* and five Jakata tales, Rabelais and Zhuangzi, Marcel Mauss and Galileo.

In the rigorously anonymous 'critical bulletin' that Claudio had in mind, the essential thing was to do battle with monsters, following the model of Rabelais, frankly and without any malice. We were convinced—and I still am—that the only possibility of creation passes through destruction. The constructive part was to be entrusted, against all false encyclopedisms, to the meticulous commentary on particular works—a poem by Cavalcanti, a passage from Spinoza, an Eskimo story, like those published by Éveline Lot-Falck which he liked so much, where, in the end, the narrator 'spits out' the story.

On the threshold of our research, Claudio wrote Valéry's phrase 'L'âge du monde fini commence' and that of Mauss: 'Même pour savoir il faut comprendre'.[39] We were thinking of a sort of comparative and annotated inventory of the essential problems at the crux of each discipline, which would for the first time allow one to understand and almost see as if on a map the phenomenon of 'man' in its entirety. And this endeavour necessarily entailed a theology—but not as an entry in the inventory; rather, as a dimension of the map.

Standing before the perspectives opened by Claudio, I had the impression of an unprecedented richness and, at the same time, the feeling of the impossibility of facing up to it. Perhaps periods of decadence, contrary to how it may seem, are just this: an excess of possibilities with respect to the ability to realize them.

On a page I happened to find, a note dated 24 May 1978: 'Meeting with Claudio. The divine and the comic. The whole sphere of the divine in the Indo-European world is comic. All the Greek gods are comic. Indo-European mythology is "comic", except the Germanic element. In the Indo-Germanic (as the Germans say) the "Germanic" is tragic and the "Indo" is comic. Hence the special situation of Hölderlin, who wants to overcome tragedy within a tragic context.' This is why, I now add, Hölderlin's translations of Sophocles' tragedies could not help but make Schiller and Goethe laugh (this in no way justifies their blindness).

If I think of the friends and people whom I have loved, it seems to me they all had in common something that I can only express in these words: what was indestructible in them was their fragility, their infinite capacity to be destroyed. But perhaps this is the most just definition of man, of that *instabilissimum animal* that, according to Dante, is man. Man has no other substance than this: the infinite ability to survive change and destruction. This remnant, this fragility is precisely what remains constant, what resists the changing vicissitudes of individual and collective history. And this remnant is the secret feature that is so hard to recognize in our changing, deciduous human faces.

This was also true of Claudio. I was astounded when I saw him—who seemed so untouched and otherworldly—willingly assume the role of éminence grise that Giulio Einaudi had entrusted to him, at a moment of grave crisis for the publishing house, as a bulwark against the weight of experts and consultants whom he could no longer control. In truth, his innocence had remained intact and he simply did not realize that Giulio was using him and would (as he did) quickly sacrifice him as soon as the moment came. When the crisis blew up, Claudio, who as éminence grise had accumulated a great number of hatreds towards him, was the first to fall, as had happened earlier when he was kicked out of Adelphi, where thanks to Bazlen he had initially played an important role (the beautiful volumes of the 'Fascicoli' series, like the one devoted to the *Grand Jeu* in 1967, have his fingerprints all over them).

While discussing our plans for a journal with Claudio, I was taking notes for a series of portraits of the great representatives of the general science of the human, which I thought I could glimpse, as in a dream, in our conversations. Aby Warburg's was the only one of these portraits that was brought to completion; of the unfinished others, the one I cared about most was to be devoted to Émile Benveniste, the linguist whose work has never ceased to accompany me since I first read it at the beginning of the seventies. In the work of this most precocious genius, who at age 22 had crossed paths with the surrealists and at 25 had succeeded Antoine Meillet at the École pratique des hautes études, comparative grammar had reached a high point on whose peak the categories of linguistic science and historical research seemed to waver and flow into philosophy. For him language was not merely a system of signs and an inventory of labels attached to things: rather, it was always the live exercise of speech, which always says and announces something to someone ('Language,' he writes in a note for his lectures at the Collège de France, nearly forced to invent non-existent words, 'is not solely *signalique*, it is *nuntial*'). And nothing testifies to this 'nunciality' of the word more than the extraordinary theory of enunciation that he developed in the last years of his life, in which the locutor, saying 'I', 'here', 'now', does not refer to the text of the enunciation but to the announcement itself and even to the voice that utters it: an 'angel', a messenger who, in saying something, above all announces himself.

At that time Italo lived with Chichita and their daughter Giovanna in a small three-story house on square de Châtillon, where Ginevra and I would often go to visit him, sometimes with Claudio. I think the common image of a rationalist and geometrical Calvino must be drastically amended. His was, rather, an extraordinary form of analogical imagination barely concealed by an enlightenment residue (owing, I think, to his youthful militancy in the Communist Party— that is, the place most lacking in imagination that then existed in Italy). The combinatory techniques that, as I recall, he employed while writing 'The Tavern of Crossed Destinies' and *Invisible Cities* belonged more to magic than to reason. To be sure, following a characteristic that has persistently marked Italian literature after Dante, who still defined himself as a philosopher, philosophy was foreign to Calvino—but this did not prevent him from exercising his analogical thought with absolute freedom in a direction that was not far from the 'nameless science' whose contours Claudio and I sought to trace. And I remember the emotion when at Lascaux— which we were able to visit in a small group of five—we suddenly found ourselves in the great hall in front of the marvellous array of bulls, horses and deer, and further on, lowering ourselves with difficulty into the tight shaft, in front of the dying man with erect phallus and the wounded bison. Perhaps only in those moments, when he finds himself suddenly transported back in time twenty thousand years, can man understand himself. Prehistory is truer than history, because it has not been transmitted by a tradition, knows no

documents, but suddenly appears like the Lascaux cave to the boy from Montignac who had slipped into it by chance. Like Claudio's, Italo's mind was able to tear the things he thought about from their context and situate them in a sort of imaginary prehistory. And what springs fresh from the source is only that knowledge which, within history, can always draw from this prehistoric dimension.

Claudio in turn had his model or teacher: Bobi Bazlen. I remember the emotion with which he told me of his last meeting with him the night before his death. Like his teacher, Claudio wanted to leave neither work nor trace—even if, as happened with Adelphi's inappropriate canonization of Bazlen, this might one day be attributed to him as a work and a trace—the trace that, like Plotinus' forms, is nothing but the imprint of the formless. Perhaps in both cases it is a fragility so extreme that for fear of failing to live up to it, it refuses to take on any form. The 'continuous repression and questioning of anything that can appear as a point of arrival' that Sergio Solmi attributed to Bazlen coincides with this fragility.

I met Bazlen only once, in Rome, in the years—probably 1962—when the publishing house Adelphi was getting off the ground. I could not help but be surprised when, while asking me about my literary preferences, he recognized my astrological sign at first sight. I think, though, that nothing ever caused him such harm as (in the words of Montale, who knew him up close) 'the untrustworthy paper legend' that has been built up around him. He was not a Taoist or Zen master but, more simply, in his own words, 'a respectable person who spends nearly all of his time in bed smoking and reading.' This accords with what Claudio told me about his refusal of the exceptional (his refusal, to be clear, of the world of Kraus, Kafka, Musil—see his incredible, and ultimately negative, reader's report on *The Man Without Qualities*) and of his pointing towards the simple and towards anthropology. As his close friends testify, he had a great and particular talent for understanding and helping other people. Elsa told me that, on a sad night when she had been strongly tempted to suicide, Bobi stayed with her on the phone continuously until he was able to persuade her to give up the idea.

In every house where I have lived, the—slightly antiquated—photograph that Elsa gave me as a keepsake has always watched over me. For the inexperienced kid who was then just starting along his path, my meeting and friendship with Elsa were an incomparable viaticum. One either entered into Elsa's circle right away or was just as irrevocably rejected. There were no initiation ceremonies, as there were in the George circle, and the criteria for entry were the most unpredictable, given that Sandro Penna and Cesare Garboli were there along with kids of all sorts, so long as they were not at all vulgar (beauty, as it was for George, was appreciated, but not indispensable). My entry was followed a few years later by the arrival of Patrizia Cavalli and Carlo Cecchi, who became more and more intimate and devoted as I started to slowly move away.

It was not, as Italo once said to me, that one could spend time with Elsa only within her cult: rather, if there was a cult, its object was not Elsa but only gods whom she had recognized as her equals or superiors. In the poem she wrote in 1967, 'Song of the H. F. and the U. M.', Elsa drew up an iconostasis of these divinities in the form of a cross.

Perhaps nowhere more than in this 'song' did Elsa so fiercely lay herself bare and conflicted, while at the same time expressing her deepest thought. For the encomium of the cheer of the Happy Few is entirely saturated with the pain felt for their dismal worldly fate— for the hospital cot where Simone Weil lay down to die, for Rimbaud's amputated leg, for the aberrant law of the prison where Gramsci was ground down. And similarly, the almost sarcastic description of the sadness of the Unhappy Many has running through it something like a countermelody of nostalgia for the lost brotherhood with the Poor Many. This is why the song should be read together with Zbigniew Herbert's poem about the temptation of Spinoza, which seems in some ways to be a secret response to it. To Spinoza, who desires only to reach God, God, absently stroking his beard,

BENEDICTUS Spinoza

(la festa del tesoro nascosto)

Morto bandito
in età di 45 anni
nel 1677

ANTONIO Gramsci
(la speranza
di una Città reale)
Morto di consunzione
carceraria
in età di 46 anni
nel 1937

SIMONA Weil

(l'intelligenza della santità)

Morta di deperimento
volontario in ospedale
in età di 34 anni
nel 1943

GIORDANO Bruno

(la grande epifania)

Bruciato vivo
in età di 52 anni
nel 1600

ARTURO Rimbaud

(l'avventura sacra)

Morto di cancrena
all'ospedale
in età di 37 anni
nel 1891

VOLFANGO A. Mozart

(la voce)

Morto di tifo
in età di 34 anni
nel 1791
sepolto col funerale
dei poveri

GIOVANNA Tarc
intesa D'Arc

(i Troni invisibili)

Bruciata viva
in età di 19 anni
nel 1431

GIOVANNI Bellini
detto Giambellino

(la salute dell'occhio,
che illumina il corpo)

Morto di vecchiezza
comune
nel 1516

PLATONE di Atene
(la lettura dei simboli)

Morto di vecchiezza
comune
nel 347 a.C.

REMBRANDT Harmensz.
van Rijn

(la luce)

Sopravvissuto
ai suoi più cari e
morto in età di 63 anni
nel 1669

recalls the small human joys that the philosopher has forgotten: 'temper / the rational fury / it will topple thrones / and blacken the stars /—think of / a woman / who will give you a child /—you see Baruch / we speak of Great Things.'[40] But the high point of the song is where Elsa, abandoning encomia and condemnations, false cheer and belied affliction, draws up the manifesto of her final thought, where philosophy and theology, as in a Buddhist mantra, collapse upon each other:

But for all legible things
there always exists another, hidden reading,
& if the living lose the code books,
so does the author of the scriptures,
even though he's called God. In fact, the living are the house
    of this one God,
so if they close their windows, the dweller in the house
will go blind.
We must open again the lights of our eyes
for him to regain his sight.
Perhaps
in heaven doesn't mean a kingdom come, nor even
an other's region. Perhaps, the double
image *on earth as it is in heaven* can be read
as one image doubled in its own mirror.
Perhaps, *turn and become like children* teaches that the ultimate
    intelligence of the end

resides in identifying with the beginning. And the mysterious
    trinity
is explained by the seed that, while begetting, begets itself
through the seamless blood of its own virgin death.
As for your *neighbour*
you (I'm speaking for you too, you half U. M. writing here)
can recognize him naturally in those who are born
nobody knows where from, & die to go nobody knows
    where
with no one to save them from grief or spare them from
    death:
no mothers or fathers on earth or in heaven.
Alone and homeless: no more, no less
than you.
And here the Anonymous cave writer is in fact sure
that in the difficult command: *Love him as thyself*
the *as* must be read as meaning *because*. BECAUSE
the *other*—the *others* (H. F. & U. M. & sapiens & faber & dog
    & toad & every other deathbound life)
ARE all yourself: not your fellows or peers or companions
    or brothers
but that same one
YOUR
SELF.[41]

Elsa was serious, savagely and tragically serious in her love for her gods, as can only be those who have made fiction ('In you, Fiction, I cloak myself / lunatic garment')[42] their privileged dwelling place. In this, the cult of poetry and beauty was no different from that which reigned in the George circle, and—as happened with Simone Weil, whom I brought to her attention—new divinities were admitted, just as she transmitted hers to us, unconditionally and unreservedly.

Even if this happened while sitting in a trattoria outside of Rome (she was particularly fond of the one called Ai trenini) or in a cafe at Trinità dei Monti, it was through her own fever, her own passion that Elsa showed me how far one can love and unconditionally believe in that truth of men and things that she at times simply called reality. (I still recall with a sort of unease that one day, while we were waiting outside the room in the clinic where she spent her last days, Moravia confided in me with candid blindness that Elsa never had a sense of reality.)

It is through Elsa, who spoke of her as an extraordinary discovery ('Patrizia is poetry,' she would say), that Patrizia entered into my life in 1970 or 1971. From that point on we have never ceased to see each other, first in Paris where we lived in those years, and then in Rome, Ponza, Venice, wherever. I have written about her poetry elsewhere, but it is as if I had spoken about her life, about her way of

being always indolently and theatrically herself—an Alexandrian poet unwillingly given over to the pompous presence of objects, to the chair that does not stop being such a chair, to the exhausted journey from the bed to the kitchen, to the cemeteries of shirts and scarves spread about every room. This is why her epigrams always end up being a lament and her mumbling always flows into a hymn. Her 'singular I, mine alone', which she so stubbornly insists upon, is not in truth an I and does not trace back to any consciousness or to any plan; it is like the single eye of a prehistoric animal that forgets itself with every bat of its eyelid. And yet, like Elsa, this antediluvian reptile is curious and, in its simple existence, unwaveringly demanding.

One summer in Ponza—one of the places where I have always been happy and, as in Scicli, hid my heart somewhere—on an afternoon when we had taken a good dose of LSD and wandered around buoyant and hallucinating in our house by the sea, Patrizia appeared suddenly and could not understand what had made us seem so distant and, at the same time, blessed. With us was Pauline, agile and slim in her model-like grace, and Patrizia questioned her until she gave up our secret. Then we went down to the harbour together for dinner and Patrizia had poetically, curiously, avidly entered into our hallucination, on that long evening in which everything—the moon, the song of the crickets, the stars—appeared as if it were for the first time.

At a certain point, late that night, we reached the beach of Chiaia di Luna, and I remember perfectly that in the enchanted contemplation of all this beauty, it seemed to me that only one thing could raise an objection to the absolute beatitude that filled my mind and senses: justice—as if the waves lapping the sand and the stars high above stubbornly repeated this one question: 'Are you just, are you just?'

It was through Elsa that I met Pasolini, who would give me the part of the apostle Philip in his *Gospel*. It now seems to me no mere chance that it was Philip, since it is with his name that a gnostic gospel that I was already reading with passion has come down to us. 'Light and darkness, life and death, right and left,' the Gospel reads, 'are siblings; it is impossible for them to separate. Accordingly, the good is not good, the bad is not bad, life is not life, death is not death.' And: 'Faith receives, love gives. No one can receive without faith, no one can give without love. Thus in order to receive we believe, and in order to love we give.' And again, 'People who say they will first die and then arise are mistaken. If they do not first receive resurrection while they are alive, once they have died they will receive nothing.'[43]

In this book—as in my life, as in every life—the dead and the living are all here together, so close and demanding that it is not easy to tell how different the presence of the living is from that of the dead. I believe the only possible meaning of the resurrection of the dead, of the *anastasis nekrōn*, is this: that we bring them back at every moment, that we are the bosom of Abraham in which, without trumpets sounding and without judgment, they ceaselessly come back to life. Nor is this merely a question of memory: memories of the dead can be sweet or bitter, but they do not entail their presence; indeed, they keep them far away in the past. This is why Etty Hillesum wanted to tear up Spier's portrait upon his death, wanted there to be nothing between her and the dead man—not even an image, not even a memory. In the eternal instant in which we are in God, there is no longer any difference between the living and the dead; we come back in them as they in us.

Loving, believing in someone or something does not mean accepting dogmas and doctrines as true. It is, rather, like remaining faithful to the emotion that one felt as a child looking up at the starry sky. And certainly in this sense I have believed in the people and things that I have gone about offhandedly recalling here one by one; I have tried not to forget them, tried to keep the word I tacitly gave. But if I now had to say where I finally put my hopes and my faith, I could only confess in a lowered voice: not in the sky above—but in the grass. In the grass—in all its forms, the tufts of slender blades, the soft clover, the lupin, the borage, the snowdrops, the dandelions, the lobelia and the calamint, but also the couch grass and nettles in all their subspecies, and the noble acanthus, which covers part of the garden where I walk every day. The grass, the grass is God. In the grass—in God—are all those whom I have loved. For the grass and in the grass and like the grass I have lived and will live.

1 Ibn Majah, *Sunan ibn Majah*, VOL. 5 (Huda Khattab ed., Nasiruddin al-Khattab trans.) (Riyadh: Darussalam, 2007), HADITH 4190.

2 *Un homme qui a quelque chose de nouveau à dire ne peut être d'abord écouté que de ceux qui l'aiment*: A man who has something new to say can only be heard at first by those who love him.

3 Nicola Chiaromonte, *The Paradox of History: Stendhal, Tolstoy, Pasternak, and Others* (Philadelphia: University of Pennsylvania Press, 1985), p. 137.

4 Nicola Chiaromonte, *Che cosa rimane: Taccuini 1955–1971* (Miriam Chiaromonte ed.) (Bologna: Il Mulino, 1995).

5 Søren Kierkegaard, *Either/Or: Part I* (Howard V. Hong and Edna H. Hong eds and trans) (Princeton, NJ: Princeton University Press, 1987), p. 27.

6 Martin Samuel Cohen, *The Shi'ur Qomah: Liturgy and Theurgy in Pre-Kabbalistic Jewish Mysticism* (Lanham: University Press of America, 1983), pp. 189, 198, 215.

7 *ce sombre dément d'Althusser*: that dark madman Althusser.

8 *homme ou cave*: man or sucker.

9 *quelques exotiques que j'ignore très regrettablement et* [. . .] *quatre ou cinq Français que je ne veux pas du tout lire*: a few exotic ones whom I very regrettably do not know and [. . .] four or five French ones whom I do not want to read at all.

10 *chianca 'e cavallo*: horse-meat butcher shop.

11 'Something happened to the people of the Western world at the beginning of the century, something quite strange: we lost science without even being aware

of it . . . ' Simone Weil, 'At the Price of an Infinite Error' in *Late Philosophical Writings* (Eric O. Springstead ed.) (Eric O. Springstead and Lawrence E. Schmidt trans) (Notre Dame: University of Notre Dame Press, 2015), p. 155.

12 Simone Weil, 'London Notebook' in *First and Last Notebooks* (Richard Rees trans.) (London: Oxford University Press, 1970), p. 352.

13 Weil, *First and Last Notebooks*, p. 358.

14 Simone Weil, 'Human Personality' in *Selected Essays, 1934–1943* (Richard Rees trans.) (London: Oxford University Press, 1962), pp. 13–14.

15 Simone Weil, *Gravity and Grace* (Arthur Wills trans.) (Lincoln: University of Nebraska Press, 1997), p. 198.

16 Al-Kisā'ī, *Tales of the Prophets* (Wheeler M. Thackston Jr. trans.) (Chicago, IL: Great Books of the Islamic World, 1997), p. 26.

17 Dante Alighieri, *The Divine Comedy of Dante Alighieri, Volume 3: Paradiso* (Robert M. Durling ed. and trans.) (New York: Oxford University Press, 2011), p. 23.

18 Dante, *Divine Comedy, Volume 3: Paradiso*, p. 603.

19 *Ego qui ad portas veni inferi et vidi*: I who came to the gates of hell and saw.

20 Carlo Bertocchi, *Confessioni minori* (Sauro Albisani ed.) (Florence: Sansoni, 1985).

21 Carlo Bertocchi, *Poesie del sabato* (Milan: Mondadori, 1985).

22 Plato, *Complete Works* (John M. Cooper ed.) (Indianapolis, IN: Hackett, 1997), p. 1646.

23 Ludwig Wittgenstein, *Culture and Value* (G. H. von Wright ed., Peter Winch trans.) (Chicago, IL: University of Chicago Press, 1980), p. 24e.

24 Translated into English as 'Shared Voices' in Gayle L. Ormiston and Alan D. Schrift (eds), *Transforming the Hermeneutic Context: From Nietzsche to Nancy* (New York: State University of New York Press, 1989).

25 Walter Benjamin, *Selected Writings, Volume 2: 1927–1934* (Michael W. Jennings, Howard Eiland and Gary Smith eds) (Rodney Livingstone et al. trans.) (Cambridge, MA: Belknap Press / Harvard University Press, 1999), p. 604.

26 Benjamin, *Selected Writings, Volume 2*, p. 384.

27 Norbert von Hellingrath, 'Hölderlins Wahnsinn' in *Zwei Vorträge: Hölderlin und die Deutschen; Hölderlins Wahnsinn* (Munich: Bruckmann, 1922), p. 23.

28 Walter Benjamin, *The Correspondence of Walter Benjamin: 1910–1940* (Gershom Scholem and Theodor W. Adorno eds) (Manfred R. Jacobson and Evelyn M Jacobson trans) (Chicago, IL: University of Chicago Press, 1994), p. 175.

29 Benjamin, *Correspondence*, p. 588.

30 Plato, *Complete Works*, pp. 1659, 1661.

31 Plato, *Complete Works*, pp. 1483–84.

32 Plato, *Complete Works*, pp. 1659.

33 Lodewijk Bolk, 'On the problem of anthropogenesis', *Proceedings of the Royal Academy* 29 (1926): 465–474.

34 Carlo Collodi, *The Adventures of Pinocchio* (Nicolas J. Perella trans.) (Berkeley, CA: University of California Press, 1986), p. 189.

35 Robert Walser, *'Masquerade' and Other Stories* (Susan Bernofsky trans.) (Baltimore, MD: Johns Hopkins University Press, 1990), p. 103.

36 Carl Seelig, *Walks with Walser* (Anne Posten trans.) (New York: New Directions, 2017), p. 40.

37 Walser, *'Masquerade' and Other Stories*, p. 168.

38 Robert Walser, *Jakob von Gunten* (Christopher Middleton trans.) (New York: New York Review Books, 1999), p. 176.

39 Valéry: *L'âge du monde fini commence*, 'The age of the finite world has begun'. Mauss: *Même pour savoir il faut comprendre*, 'Even to know one has to understand'.

40 Zbigniew Herbert, *The Collected Poems 1956–1998* (Alissa Valles ed. and trans.) (New York: Ecco Press, 2007), pp. 315–16.

41 Elsa Morante, *The World Saved by Kids and Other Epics* (Cristina Viti trans.) (London: Seagull Books, 2016), pp. 185–87.

42 Elsa Morante, *Lies and Sorcery* (Jenny McPhee trans.) (New York: New York Review Books, 2023), p. 1.

43 *The Gnostic Scriptures* (Bentley Layton trans.) (Garden City: Doubleday, 1987), pp. 330, 337, 345.

ILLUSTRATIONS

PAGE *ii*. Studio, San Polo 2366, Venice, 2007. Photograph by Pedro Paixão. Courtesy of the photographer.

PAGE 2. Paul Gaugin, *Autoportrait (près du Golgotha)*, 1896.

PAGE 5. Studio, San Polo, 2016. Photograph by Giorgio Agamben.

PAGE 6. Studio, Vicolo del Giglio 2A, Rome, 1987. Photograph by Giorgio Agamben.

PAGE 8. Detail of the studio, San Polo, 2016. Photograph by Giorgio Agamben.

PAGE 10. Martin Heidegger and the author, Thouzon, 1966. Photograph by François Fédier. Courtesy of the photographer.

PAGE 11. The participants of the seminar at Le Thor on a walk, Thouzon, 1966. Photograph by François Fédier. Courtesy of the photographer.

PAGE 13. Ramón Gaya, *Autorretrato con metrónomo*, 1979. © DACS, 2024.

PAGES 14–15. Postcards from Martin Heidegger to the author.

PAGE 16. Martin Heidegger, the author and others, Le Thor, 1968. Photograph by François Fédier. Courtesy of the photographer.

PAGE 17. Martin Heidegger, the author, René Char, Jean Beaufret and Dominique Fourcade among pétanque players, 1966. Photograph by François Fédier. Courtesy of the photographer.

PAGE 18. Postcard from the author to Giovanni Urbani, Le Thor, 1966.

PAGE 20. (*Left to right*) Alberto Moravia, Ginevra Bompiani, the author, Kiki Brandolini, Giovanni Urbani, Dacia Maraini, Ilaria Occhini and Raffaele La Capria, August 1966.

PAGE 23. The participants of the seminar at Le Thor, 1966 (*Left to right*: Dominique Fourcade, François Vezin, Ginevra Bompiani, Martin Heidegger, Jean Beaufret and the author).

PAGE 24. (*Standing, left to right*) Heinrich Blücher, Hannah Arendt, Dwight McDonald and Gloria McDonald; (*seated*) Nicola Chiaromonte, Mary McCarthy and Robert Lowell; New York, 1966. Courtesy of the Vassar College Library and *BOMB*.

PAGE 29. Studio, Vicolo del Giglio, 1987. Photograph by Giorgio Agamben.

PAGE 31. Photograph of Herman Melville.

PAGE 35. Advertising leaflet of the Verre à Pied, rue Mouffetard, Paris.

PAGE 36. Farmhouse of Montechiarone, Siena, 1980. Photograph by Giorgio Agamben.

PAGE 39. Photograph from the window of the studio, Vicolo del Giglio, 1987, by Giorgio Agamben.

PAGE 41. (*Left*) The author in the studio at Piazza delle Coppelle 48. Rome, 1967. (*Right*) Cover of Friedrich Hölderlin, *Scritti sulla poesia e frammenti* (Turin: Boringhieri, 1958).

PAGE 43. Ingeborg Bachmann as a girl. Courtesy of the Ingeborg Bachmann Photo Archive.

PAGE 45. Map of Rome, Piazza delle Coppelle and surroundings.

PAGE 49. Cover of Simone Weil, *Écrits de Londres et dernières lettres* (Paris: Gallimard, 1957).

PAGE 52. Photograph of José Bergamín by Giorgio Agamben.

PAGE 53. Page annotated by José Bergamín in Simone Weil's *Écrits de Londres et dernières lettres*.

PAGE 54. (*Above*) Manuscript by José Bergamín, 1982. (*Below*) José Bergamín and the author, Seville, 1976. Photo by Ginevra Bompiani.

PAGE 56. José Bergamín and the author, Seville, 1976. Photograph by Ginevra Bompiani.

PAGE 59. Photograph of José Bergamín.

PAGE 61. (*Left to right*) The author, Isabel Quintanilla and Francisco López, Castelgandolfo, 1962.

PAGE 62. Isabel Quintanilla, *Cuarto de baño*, 1968. © DACS, 2024.

PAGE 63. Francisco López, *Bodegón con membrillos*, 1973. Courtesy of the Brockstedt Hans Galerie, Hamburg.

PAGE 64. The author in the apartment in the Casin de' Nobili, Dorsoduro 2763, Venice, 1996. Photograph by Mario Dondero. Courtesy of the photographer.

PAGE 65. Martina.

PAGE 66. Casin de' Nobili, Venice.

PAGE 68. *Cupid Riding a Snail over Fungus Vegetation*, 1524.

PAGE 69. Titian, *Flaying of Marsyas*, 1570-1576.

PAGE 70. Avigdor Arikha, *Due pietre*, 1977. Courtesy of the estate of Avigdor Arikha.

PAGE 71. Sonia Alvarez, *Blanket and Beadspread*, 2009. Courtesy of Galleria Tecnica Mista, Scicli.

PAGE 72. Monica Ferrando, *Kore*, 2000. Photograph by Davide Ghaleb. Courtesy of the photographer.

PAGE 74. Detail of the studio, Vicolo del Giglio, 1987. Photograph by Giorgio Agamben.

PAGE 75. Notebook with notes by the author.

PAGE 76. Detail of the studio, San Polo, 2007. Photograph by Pedro Paixão. Courtesy of the photographer.

PAGE 78. Original manuscript of 'Ritorno' by Giorgio Caproni, 1978.

PAGES 80–81. Detail of the studio, San Polo, 2016. Photograph by Giorgio Agamben.

PAGE 85. Postcard from Alfred Jarry, 1907. Photograph by Pedro Paixão. Courtesy of the photographer.

PAGE 86. Photograph of Alfred Jarry.

PAGE 89. Cover of René Crevel, *Êtes-vous fous?* (Paris: Gallimard, Paris).

PAGE 90. Page from René Crevel, *Êtes-vous fous?*.

PAGE 91. *Le père Ubu*, lithograph by Pierre Bonnard, from Ambroise Vollard, *Le père Ubu à l'hôpital* (Paris, 1918).

PAGE 92. Pierre Bonnard, *Nu rose, tête ombrée, c.* 1919.

PAGE 94. Jean-Luc and Hélène Nancy with the author in the Sienese countryside (late 1980s).

PAGE 95. Manuscript of a dream by Walter Benjamin.

PAGE 97. Poems by Friedrich Heinle. Manuscript copy by Carla Seligson.

PAGE 100. Helen Hessel, photographed in Paris, *c.* 1929. Marianne Breslauer © Walter & Konrad Feilchenfeldt / Fotostiftung Schweiz.

PAGE 101. Villa Discoboli, Capri, 1981. Photograph by Giorgio Agamben.

PAGE 102. Jean Selz, his wife Guyet and Walter Benjamin in Ibiza, 1933.

PAGE 103. Walter Benjamin's last address in Paris, 10 rue Dombasle. Photograph by Giorgio Agamben.

PAGE 105. Note written by Walter Benjamin on the back of a letter from Jean Wahl.

PAGE 105. Fragment of a letter from Jean Wahl to Walter Benjamin.

PAGE 106. Note written by Walter Benjamin.

PAGE 108. Stefan George with Claus Berthold von Stauffenberg, Berlin, 1924. Courtesy of the Stefan George Archive.

PAGE 109. Cover of Max Kommerell, *Der Dichter als Führer in der deutschen Klassik* (Berlin: Bondi, 1928).

PAGE 111. Pivetta once belonging to Bruno Leone.

PAGE 113. Norbert von Hellingrath with girlfriend Imma von Ehrenfels, Munich, 1915.

PAGE 116. Photograph of Giorgio Pasquali.

PAGE 121. Detail of the studio, Vicolo del Giglio, 1987. Photo by Giorgio Agamben.

PAGE 121. Detail of the studio, Via Corsini 14A, Rome, 2016. Photograph by Giorgio Agamben.

PAGE 123. Photograph of Bianca Casalini Agamben.

PAGE 124. Detail of the studio, San Polo, 2015. Photograph by Giorgio Agamben.

PAGE 125. Giovanni Serodine, *Allegory of Science*, c. 1625.

PAGE 128. With Maresa Scodanibbio in Mexico, November 1995. Photograph by Stefano Scodanibbio.

PAGE 130. Page from the notebooks of Sandro M.

PAGE 131. The cantaores Enrique Montes and Pies de Plomo (*centre*), Seville, 1992.

PAGE 132. Detail of the library of the studio, San Polo. Photo by Giorgio Agamben.

PAGE 133. Photograph of Giorgio Colli by Mario Cappelletti.

PAGE 136. (*Above*) Illustration from the *Alfabeto della signorina Mimí* (Milan: Tipografica editrice lombarda, 1877). (*Below*) Illustration from a Greek ABC book.

PAGES 139–40. Illustrations by Sabino Profeti from Tommaso Landolfi, *Il principe infelice* (Florence: Vallecchi, 1943).

PAGE 143. (*Above*) Photograph of Robert Walser in Herisau by Carl Seelig. Courtesy of the Robert Walser Foundation. (*Below*) Johann George Schreiner, *Friedrich Hölderlin in the Tower in Tübingen*, 1823.

PAGE 144. Illustration by Karl Walser from Robert Walser, *Gedichte* (Berlin: B. Cassirer, 1918).

PAGE 149. Ginevra and Claudio Rugafiori in Lerici, September 1973. Photograph by Giorgio Agamben.

PAGE 151. Typescript with notes by Claudio Rugafiori for a planned journal.

PAGES 154–55. Detail of the studio, San Polo, 2016. Photograph by Giorgio Agamben.

PAGE 159. Detail of cave painting in the Lascaux cave.

PAGE 161. (*Left to right*) Bobi Bazlen, Paola Olivetti, Flavia and Giovanni Colacicchi, Eugenio Montale, Elsa Morante and a friend in Forte dei Marmi, 1941.

PAGE 163. From Elsa Morante, *La canzone degli F. P. e degli I. M.* (1968).

PAGE 166. Elsa Morante (1940s). Courtesy of Foto Barzanti.

PAGE 168. The author with Patrizia Cavalli, 1984.

PAGE 169. Business card of Casa Vitiello, Ponza.

PAGE 170. (*Left to right*) Pier Paolo Pasolini, Enrique Irazoqui, Giacomo Morante and the author on the set of *Il Vangelo secondo Matteo*, 1964. Courtesy Cineteca di Bologna / Fondo Angelo Novi.

PAGE 172. Photograph by Giorgio Agamben.